SUMMER OF THE DUDES

Book Three:
The Dudes Adventure Chronicles

By Tyler Reynolds

And Emily Johnson

Epic Spiel Press

This work is a work of fiction. Names, characters, places, and incidents are the product of the author's imagination or are used fictitiously. Any resemblance to actual events, locales, or persons, living or dead, is coincidental.

Text copyright © 2019 Emily Kay Johnson

Cover illustration copyright © 2019 Jacquelyn B. Moore

ISBN-13: 978-1-949212-06-8

All Rights Reserved. In accordance with the U.S. Copyright Act of 1976, the scanning, uploading, and electronic sharing of any part of this book without the permission of the publisher is unlawful piracy and theft of the author's intellectual property.

Thank you for your support of the author's rights.

This book is also available in print at amazon.com

Epic Spiel Press

To Braxton, Drew, Natalie, Grant, Grace, and Trent who make epic adventures for their parents to remember.

And to Boomer, Bret, Rachel, Erin, Kate, and Mary, who are pretty epic despite having grown up.

The Dudes Adventure Chronicles

Save the Dudes

Dudes Take Over

Summer of the Dudes

Dudes in the Middle–*coming soon!*

Check them out at **thedudeschronicles.com**

Table of Contents

1 Dudes All Wet 7
2 Dudes At Sea 19
3 Dude Territory 30
4 Dudes Overshoot 38
5 Dudes Dart Down 45
6 Dudes Save the Day 53
7 Dudes Make a Splash 66
8 Dudes Shake It Up 77
9 Dude Quake 87
10 Dudes Prepared 97
11 Dudes Serve the Public 108
12 Dudes Safe Room 116
13 A Dudes Production 122
14 Dudes About Town 132
15 Dudes Invasion 140
16 Dudes Power Down 147
17 Dudes Offline 154
18 Dudevision 162
19 The Dudes and the Bear 169
20 Cryptid Hunter Dudes 179

1 Dudes All Wet

If you're reading this Chronicle, be prepared for some epic adventures. And, when I say "epic" I mean Zombie Playground Incident and Great Elephant Caper epic. That's why I keep the Chronicles of the Dudes, so what we've done will never be forgotten.

Sure, right now we're just average about-to-be 6th graders. But someday, when people read of our exploits, they'll think of us as champions of our generation.

I was thinking that very thing when I arrived at Ryan and Connor's house one morning in June to discover them zip-tied together.

Nate and Deven had already arrived so the five Dudes were all there: Tyler Reynolds (that's me), Nate Howe, Deven Singh, and Ryan and Connor Maguire.

Ryan and Connor are twins, by the way, which didn't make it easier to explain their situation.

"We were watching *Like the Law* on mom's laptop," Ryan began, rubbing his brush of reddish blonde hair with his left hand and practically poking himself in the eye with Connor's right hand, which happened to be attached to it.

Connor jumped off the tool bench, jerking Ryan forward in the process. "They had to arrest a bunch of perps in a garage," he said. (In case you didn't know, *Like the Law* was online cop videos.)

"Let me tell it," Ryan demanded. "They were taking apart these stolen cars," he explained.

"The bad guys," Connor put in.

Ryan glared at him. "And they didn't have enough handcuffs," he said.

"The cops didn't," Connor interrupted.

"So they used zip ties from the garage," said Ryan.

"They used the crooks' own zip ties!" crowed Connor, throwing his right hand in the air, which yanked Ryan's left hand which, in turn, caused Ryan to use his right hand to sock his twin in the stomach.

"Anyway, we came out to see if *we* had any zip ties," said Ryan.

"And decided to arrest yourselves?" I finished for him.

1 Dudes All Wet

"You really *can't* get out of them," said Connor, demonstrating by pulling on the end of the tie.

"You just made it tighter, dufus!" said Ryan.

Connor stared down at his hand. "Whoa, I think my fingers are going numb."

"You'll wish you were numb!" warned Ryan.

"Your thumbs are turning purple," Nate observed with scientific interest.

It was about that time that Ryan and Connor's dad drove up and parked his motorcycle in the driveway. When he saw how things were, he sighed and said, "I hope you didn't do this until *after* your mom left for work."

Ryan and Connor's mom and dad are divorced. That morning, Mrs. Maguire had carpooled to work so she could leave the minivan for our river trip. I guess Mr. Maguire didn't think this was a great start.

"You're making me look bad here, dudes," he said. (He's the only one of our parents who ever calls us that.) "I was the one who convinced your mom that you didn't need day camps this summer because I'm only teaching two days a week at the community college. I swore you'd be fine supervising yourselves whenever I wasn't around."

"Then I guess it's a good thing you're around today. Huh, Dad?" said Ryan.

Mr. Maguire grabbed the scissors off the tool bench and cut the zip ties—a solution which I'm sure would have occurred to Ryan and Connor eventually.

"Everybody get in the van," ordered Mr. Maguire.

We all climbed into the minivan, but the lecture wasn't over.

"You have too much time on your hands and not enough to do," said Mr. Maguire as he drove us out of Sherwood.

But I didn't believe it. The Dudes had done plenty of stuff (hence, the Chronicles). If anything, summer wasn't long enough to do all the stuff we could think of.

Mr. Maguire used the drive to the river to lay down some summer rules.

"No more watching *Like the Law*," he said. "No more *Kitchen Kaboom* either," he added, prompting Nate to point out that those videos display real scientific content.

Mr. Maguire shook his head. "No *Guys Gone Goofy*," he continued.

"But that's my favorite show!" moaned Deven.

1 Dudes All Wet

Mr. Maguire clenched his fingers around the wheel of the minivan. "And definitely not *Extreme Martial Arts Stunts!*" he said.

"That one's totally fake anyway, Dad," said Ryan. "They gotta be using movie special effects or something. I can prove it if you let Connor go on the roof again..."

Mr. Maguire ignored that. "I want you to stay away from online videos completely," he said. "I think I'd rather you spend your time playing some nice violent video games."

"All summer?" Connor asked.

"But it's only the first week!" Ryan protested.

Mr. Maguire nodded. "And that goes for *all* of you," he added, lowering his sunglasses to glare at us in the rearview mirror. "Your parents will thank me."

He sighed as we left the highway and began to climb a mountain road that twisted through evergreen forest. "I used to come up here every summer when I was a kid," he said, leaning his head back against the headrest. "Today I'm gonna introduce you to natural wonders."

The Dudes groaned.

"Trust me," said Mr. Maguire. "It's a perfect day to be on the river. The sun is out. There's plenty of water from the spring melt. And with that new raft I bought, you guys should have smooth sailing."

Then he frowned. "Nobody brought any zip ties did you?" he asked.

"Actually," Nate mused, "swimming while handcuffed together might be a good test of ambidexterity."

"Huh?" said Deven.

"Or a good way to drown each other," I pointed out.

"Hey, boys," said Mr. Maguire. "As we round this curve, take a look back down the mountain."

We all turned around in our seats to see a notch in the trees and a ribbon of flat, treeless green stretching through the forest, down this hill, over the next, and on toward the west. All along the ribbon, electric towers stood like robots, carrying bundles of power lines on their broad metal shoulders.

"There's a hydroelectric dam up here that turns the power of the river into electric power for the city," Mr. Maguire explained.

"Without producing greenhouse gases or other pollutants," Nate added approvingly.

1 Dudes All Wet

"Doesn't it electrocute the fish?" asked Connor. He seemed disappointed when Nate said no.

"Why are we stopping?" asked Ryan.

"I thought you guys would want to see the falls," said Mr. Maguire.

We all climbed out and watched from a balcony as water plunged over a cliff and fell 270 feet into a rocky pool below. It was pretty spectacular.

Back in the van, Deven mimed going over the falls in a minivan, which kept us distracted until Mr. Maguire turned into a dirt parking lot where his girlfriend, Tina, was waiting beside her truck.

Mr. Maguire heaved two inner tubes and a huge inflatable boat out of the pickup.

"You guys carry this stuff to the beach," he said, setting the cooler down between Ryan and Connor. "Tina and I will be back in a few minutes after we drop off the van."

It turns out, riding the river is sort of complicated. You drive up the hill to drop your people and gear at the put-in spot. Then you drive down the hill to park one car at the pull-*out* point. Then you drive back up the hill to the put-*in* spot and park the second car there. Then, after you ride the river, two drivers have to go back up the hill to reclaim the second car.

Of course, Mr. Maguire and Tina had already figured out all this stuff as well as inflating the tubes and raft and packing a cooler of sodas.

The put-in beach was where the river made a bend and a bunch of silt and rocks had collected. All over the wide, flat area, people were pumping rafts, spraying sunscreen, and loading coolers.

Nate was spraying sunscreen too—on his shins, which were about the only spot left uncovered. He was also wearing long sleeves and a swimsuit that reached his knees.

"This fabric is spf 100," he informed us, putting on a wide-brimmed hat and his green sports goggles which were polarized for glare protection.

"This hat is 100% thirst quenching!" said Deven, pulling two sodas out of the cooler and setting them in the drink holders that hung over his ears.

I noticed Ryan was happy with his usual Indiana Jones-type adventure hat, and I was making do with plain old hair.

1 Dudes All Wet

"There seem to be a wide variety of rafts," said Nate, looking around.

He wasn't kidding. There were tubes and air mattresses and boats. There were lounges with backrests and cup holders. There were inflatable kayaks and floating coolers. Six college kids scrambled onto something that had couches and foot rests and even a "hot tub" which was a reservoir lined with black rubber so the sun could warm the water in the tub while you floated along the cold river. Another group had their own floating island with a rubber palm tree and an inflatable "mountain" to slide off into the water.

There were rafts that looked like things too—the usual sea horses and orcas, sure, but also a Star Trek command chair and a giant inflatable smart phone. Giant food was a whole category. I saw a hot dog, a giant ice cream sandwich, and a slice of pepperoni pizza.

"I'm hungry," said Connor.

"You need a snack hat," suggested Deven.

When Tina and Mr. Maguire came back, they found the Dudes watching Nate design one in the sand.

"It will have a straw for liquid or gellied items," Nate explained.

"Pudding!" shouted Deven, high-fiving Connor.

"Why does it look like Connor is getting smacked in the face?" I asked, pointing to a hand shape that covered the mouth of the wearer.

"The solid food feeding device will have to mimic Connor's own usual food delivery method," Nate explained, adding, "I'll probably spring-load it."

"Hey, Dudes!" called Mr. Maguire from the water. "You going on the river today?"

He and Tina were already in their old-school inner tubes, floating peacefully with their feet up and sodas in their hands.

The Dudes grabbed the handles on our six-man inflatable boat, which we had dubbed the *S.S. Dudes,* and headed for the water. Of course, there are only five Dudes, but the sixth space was set aside for the drinks cooler.

"Leave no man behind!" Deven shouted as we stopped to heave the cooler into the raft.

And then we were off.

1 Dudes All Wet

...Well, not exactly. See the put-in beach was one side of a lagoon, and there was sort of a jam-up of rafts waiting to get out to where the current was moving on the river.

While we were waiting, I saw a man throw a tennis ball for his dog, who jumped out of the raft after it.

Then I heard a splash and saw that Connor had done the same thing. Only he wasn't chasing a ball but swimming for the far bank where there was a rope swing!

We all scrambled up the slimy mud bank and took turns swinging way out over the lagoon to drop in feet first with a splash.

Deven's splash was followed by a groan.

"I forgot about my Sunny Sip!" he cried, frowning from beneath the hat's dripping brim.

I helped him retrieve the water-logged soda cans before they sank.

"Hey, where's Dad?" asked Ryan.

I glanced toward the river, but Mr. Maguire and Tina were almost gone.

"I see them," said Connor. "They're just ahead of that yellow boat with no one in it."

"Wait a minute, that's *our* yellow boat!" shouted Ryan. "Come on, guys, swim for your lives!"

2 Dudes At Sea

"Leave no man behind!" Deven called desperately to the cooler where it crouched in the stern of our rapidly disappearing boat.

It was a lucky thing Deven's mom had made him take all those swim lessons at the Country Club. He got to the S.S. Dudes first and dragged it backwards into the lagoon until the rest of us could catch up and scramble aboard.

When all Dudes were present and accounted for, Ryan shouted, "Anchors aweigh!"

At first, the *S.S. Dudes* whirled around in the middle of the river. But when Ryan and Connor stopped paddling on the same side, we straightened out and started moving downstream with the current.

As we picked up speed, everybody took a break and got sodas out of the cooler.

Deven re-filled his hat—one side cola and one side orange drink.

"They mix in my mouth," he said. "I call it orangeola!"

It was about that time that I saw a boulder sticking out of the water ahead of us. The others hardly had time to look before…

"Whoa!"

The raft bumped the rock and dodged to the side, spinning as it slid down a drop into foamy white water.

"Not a bad ride!" I said.

"We may get some excitement after all," said Nate.

Unfortunately, when the raft dodged, Connor's hand had jerked, and root beer had splashed out of his can onto the side of Ryan's face.

"Hey! Watch it!" said Ryan, whacking him with his hat.

"Watch what?" said Connor with a grin. "This?"

He snapped his wrist forward, sending a whip of soda toward his twin.

"You asked for it," warned Ryan. Grabbing a paddle, he chipped it into the water just perfectly to throw a wave over the bow of the boat…and over Connor's face.

Connor dropped his soda in the boat and grabbed his own paddle to return fire.

"That was predictable," observed Nate, leaning against the cooler as he sipped his cola.

"Yeah, kinda boring," I agreed.

"Not with orangeola," argued Deven, taking a long sip.

But suddenly a fat stream of water hit Deven in the cans, knocking the Sunny Sip right off his head and into his lap.

"My orangeola!" Deven cried, looking around. "What happened to my orangeola? Ack! I'm leaking orangeola!"

"Stop saying orangeola!" yelled Ryan just before another blast smacked *him* in the mouth.

A third shot hit Nate in the back as the rest of us tried to duck behind the cooler.

"Sneak attack!" shouted Connor in outrage. "Where's it coming from?"

"There," said Nate, pointing behind us toward a kid a couple years younger who was riding an inflatable hot dog. He was carrying what could only be the Splashshot 3000 with pump action.

I knew that gun and disdained it. The clips held so little water. In a backyard, you were out of action in no time. But here on the river, running out of water was the least of his worries. In fact, I could see the kid had made a modification—he'd taken off the clip and attached an extension hose to the tube. The hose was long enough to drag below the hot dog, basically making the whole river his ammo clip.

"Why didn't *I* think of that?" said Nate.

"It's a battle dog," yelled Deven, "a hound of hell, a sniper sausage!"

"It's coming up fast," Nate reported.

Unfortunately, with its streamlined shape, the hot dog was traveling faster than we were. As it passed, the foe spattered our starboard side.

We all lunged to that side to get our hands in the water and try to splash him back. But the boat tipped dangerously, and we had to throw ourselves back to the center.

Then our adversary aimed at the sky and squeezed off several high lobs that landed like shells right in the boat with us.

"Take cover!" yelled Ryan, throwing himself over the far side of the raft. The rest of us followed, basically dunking ourselves.

The river was pretty shallow right there, so we had to stoop to hide behind our boat as the little boy on the hot dog sailed past laughing. Behind him, two guys on a double tube raised their colas to us as they floated by.

"Great. We're the laughing stock of the river," I said.

"That blasted bratwurst!" hollered Deven.

"This cannot stand!" promised Ryan, shaking his fist.

"We have no weapons," Connor pointed out. "Why didn't we think of bringing weapons?"

Before getting back in the boat, we decided to tip it to dump out the orangeola. While Nate held the cooler and Deven held the paddles, the rest of us pulled from one side and turned the raft over on top of ourselves.

That wasn't exactly intentional, but it was really cool. The raft enclosed an air-filled space above our heads where Nate and Deven soon joined us. It was sort of like being in a submarine, if submarines smelled like soda.

"Dudes," said Ryan, "are you thinking what I'm thinking?"

"That orangeola might mutate the fish?" I guessed.

"No!" said Ryan. "That this is the perfect cover to sneak up on that hot dog."

"Yeah!" We all agreed, and then realized that the space was way too small for yelling in.

"We'll call this Operation Sink the Brat," said Ryan more softly.

Walking on the rocky river bottom was slow and hard on the feet. So we learned to raise our legs and let the river's current push the raft along and us with it.

Unfortunately, Nate couldn't hold the cooler forever. And, after a while, the air got stale. So we all popped back up to the surface just in time to see that the river had branched.

The hot dog was nowhere in sight, but I could see a large sand bar or maybe a small island in the middle of the river. The other rafts all seemed to be taking the stream that went to the right around the island. But the Dudes were too far to the left to switch lanes now.

We decided to turn the raft back over and ride until we could catch up with our nemesis.

As we floated along, the island got big enough to support real trees. Bleached driftwood lay like piled bones along its shore. The stream was getting narrower and faster too.

"I wonder when this stream will join up again with the main river," I said nervously.

Nate answered, "It's possible that this is not a branch but a completely separate stream."

"You mean it might never join up with the other river?" asked Connor.

"Where will it take us?" I asked.

"How will we find Dad?" asked Ryan.

And then Deven said, "Hey guys, what's that rushing noise?"

Sure enough, we could now hear what sounded like rushing water—a lot of rushing water. We couldn't see what was around the bend of the stream, but the rushing sound was definitely getting closer.

"The power plant!" said Ryan.

"The waterfall!" said Connor at the same time.

Ryan and Connor grabbed the paddles and started to cut water. The rest of us lunged over the side and paddled with our hands.

"Make for the island!" shouted Ryan, steering us in that direction.

It wasn't long before we were dragging the *S.S. Dudes* onto land, and then staggering up the rocky beach.

"What do we do now?" asked Connor, panting.

"Simple," said Ryan. "We gather firewood, boil water, make an S-O-S signal out of colored stones, and sharpen sticks to prepare for attack by headhunters."

Yep, if you have to be stranded on a desert island, Ryan's the guy to have along.

Then Nate said, "Perhaps first we should attempt to reach the other stream."

He had a point. Even counting the time we spent under the raft, it couldn't be that far away.

"If we climb to a high point of the island, we should be able to get our bearings," Nate suggested.

So Ryan led us uphill over some sharp gravel, into and out of a blackberry thicket, and through a cloud of mosquitoes. Finally, we reached a small stand of fir trees at the peak of the island.

"Look!" said Connor pointing to our left.

We were on a rocky cliff about twenty feet above the water. And from our high vantage point we could see what happened to the stream we had come down—what would have happened to us if we hadn't scrambled out when we did…

We would simply have floated under the highway overpass (which was the source of the rushing sound we heard) and rejoined the main river and the other floaters just in time to reach the pull-out spot where we could see people dragging their floats out of the water.

Nate and Deven and I grinned in relief. But Ryan had turned and was looking down the cliff where we stood: straight down to where a flat rock stretched out into the river below us, and where someone had parked a giant hot dog.

"The enemy is here," whispered Ryan through clenched teeth.

The hot dog lay half in the water. The Splashshot 3000 lay in the sun beside it. But where was the boy?

Then we heard a scratchy noise coming from the base of the cliff.

Leaning over, we could see a beach where the boy was making a sand castle. It was perfect. The kid had obviously been out of the water for a while. He was nice and dry and hot.

The Dudes went into ninja mode, and Ryan led us back to the boat, where Nate used the raft pump to make a few alterations to Deven's Sunny Sip. Then we sank into the water like crocodiles, and made our way around the far end of the island.

When we reached the flat rock, we crawled out of the water on our hands and knees like commandoes.

At Ryan's signal, Connor and I worked the pump to force river water through the sippy straws. Meanwhile, Ryan aimed Deven's head like a machine gun, spraying the beach from one end to the other.

It was awesome! Hot dog boy jumped ten feet when the cold water hit him.

But suddenly, from behind us, came a deep voice: "Sneak attack!"

It was those two guys who had laughed at us. They must have been sitting in the shadow of the cliff where we couldn't see them. And they must be the kid's parents because one of them grabbed up the Splashshot 3000 and started firing.

We knew when we were outgunned.

"Retreat!" ordered Ryan.

The Dudes stumbled over each other in our haste to climb the hill where the Splashshot couldn't follow without losing its ammo supply.

We made it safely back to the S.S. Dudes and shoved off, vowing never to return—to the island, that is. We'll definitely be going on the river again. And next time, we'll be better armed.

3 Dude Territory

Ryan and Connor had some unsupervised time that summer. But I wasn't so lucky. My mom is big on supervision.

When Mom went back to work, Dad quit his job to stay home and have more family time. That would be great, except that he kept *trying* to work full-time in the home office he made out of a shed in the back yard. And, that summer, he had a big project due in August.

When school ended for the summer, Dad had a plan for us kids to "make our own fun" while he worked. The problem was that my baby brother, Leon, is only one year old, so his idea of fun is falling down stairs and choking on things and smothering himself and drowning. (At least that's what Mom seems to think.)

Also, for some reason, Mom told Dad he couldn't hire the Dudes to babysit Leon, even though we'd proved in the past we would be totally good at it (see Book 2 of the Chronicles).

Anyway, after the Dudes came back from our river trip, Dad suggested we could at least keep Jayden busy for him.

"Then I can watch Leon and plan my new work project at the same time!" Dad said confidently. Leon had just learned to walk, and it's basically all he wanted to do, so Dad got some exercise that day following him around the house and yard, ready to catch him if he fell or stop him from putting junk in his mouth.

He had a big vocabulary of weird sounds (Leon, not Dad). Come to think of it, so does Deven. Mom says, in Leon's case, they're pieces of words that he's learning how to say, and one day he'll put them all together and talk.

Meanwhile, the Dudes supervised ourselves and Jayden in our treehouse dojo. Every once in a while we would see Leon and Dad waddle by, Leon jabbering away and Dad mumbling to himself about his project.

The Dudes and I had no trouble keeping Jayden busy. But, that night, Jayden had to go and blab to Mom about reaching level seventeen playing Manic Manic Meatball

Meatball on Deven's phone. Which prompted Mom to give her speech about limiting screen time for the good of our young minds.

Besides that, it turns out there is not a lot of Dad's work that can be done while walking around stooped over with a wet pacifier in his hand. Which is why after that first day he called Grandad to take care of Leon, Jayden, and me for the summer.

Grandad came over the next morning at the crack of eleven and dragged us out of bed to go to his house. I have great memories of learning woodworking in Grandad's garage. He's got a tool bench and racks of wood, and he never complains about you wasting nails by bending them. I made this great birdhouse one time…

…well, I almost finished it. In fact, it was still sitting there on a shelf in Grandad's garage waiting for me to put on three more walls and a roof. Maybe I'd get around to finishing that this summer.

Only not right now. I wanted to type my story of the Dudes' river rafting trip into the Chronicle while the details were still fresh (and Mom wasn't around to complain about the screen time). That's when I realized I'd forgotten to bring my laptop with me!

Grandad has a computer, but, of course, Jayden was using it to download a free copy of Manic Manic Meatball Meatball.

So Grandad drove us all home. We got my laptop and had almost made it back when Grandad realized Jayden was still wearing pajamas.

So we went back to get shorts and a t-shirt for Jayden.

Then we went back again to get Leon's little tennis shoes, which he couldn't remember for himself even though walking was really his only plan for the day.

All that riding in the car made Leon fall asleep. But when Grandad tried to put him down for a nap he fell awake again. Grandad had to rock him and sing his high school anthem until Leon was asleep on his shoulder.

Anyway, you can see we were pretty busy in the morning. But, by afternoon, there was nothing for Jayden to do. The only toys Grandad had were a checker set and his computer, and Manic Manic Meatball Meatball had crashed the computer.

Grandad tried to convince Jayden that checkers were like flat meatballs, but he didn't buy it.

"I want to hammer," Jayden said.

Jayden knew how to hammer. Last year, when Mom and Dad went out for their anniversary, Grandad gave Jayden a big bag of nails and let him hammer them into an old stump in the yard. Jayden hammered on that stump until he'd used up every nail. But, since then, I guess, Grandad had bought some more.

I followed them out to the garage where I perched on the hood of Grandad's truck. (He keeps it weirdly clean, so I wasn't getting bug guts on my pants or anything.)

Grandad showed Jayden a stack of scrap lumber.

"What would you like to make?" Grandad asked.

"A spiral staircase," Jayden answered promptly.

Grandad tottered a little. "A spiral staircase?" he asked.

Jayden nodded. "I need it to get from the top of my supercave to the underground part," he explained.

I looked up from my laptop to see the look on Grandad's face. Since the supercave was currently a tent made of blankets draped over exercise equipment in our basement, I wasn't sure what Mom was going to say about Jayden digging another level.

But Grandad didn't flinch.

"Good idea, Jayden," he said, giving me a wink. "But let's start with something simpler that we know we can finish."

(I couldn't help wondering if he was thinking about my birdhouse.)

Then Grandad looked through his rack of leftover wood pieces and found two short ones and one long. He showed Jayden how to build a bench by placing the long piece just right and hammering the nails down into the leg pieces.

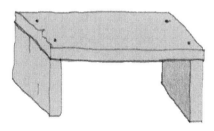

"Wow! Furniture!" said Jayden.

In a minute, though, we could hear Leon yelling word pieces and Grandad had to go in the house.

While Grandad was gone, I worked on the Chronicle and Jayden kept hammering.

I guess Grandad had to change a diaper or something. Anyway, by the time he came back carrying Leon, Jayden had completed about a dozen benches and used up every piece of scrap wood in the garage. There were short, wide benches and tall, skinny ones and plenty where the legs weren't even the same size.

"Can you make this one uncrooked?" Jayden asked.

Grandad shrugged and put Leon down so he could saw about three inches off one of the legs without sawing anything off one of his grandkids.

In the meantime, Leon stuck his hands up under the fender of the truck and found the only place that wasn't clean. He ended up with black grease all over himself.

Grandad doesn't have baby bath, so he decided we had to take Leon home to wash him. And, when Jayden announced that next he would *paint* his benches, Grandad loaded them in the truck and decided to take care of us in our own territory for the rest of the summer.

3 Dude Territory

Dad didn't care as long as we stayed out of *his* territory—the shed.

And that's how I ended up back in the dojo all summer, hanging out with the Dudes.

 ## 4 Dudes Overshoot

Jayden spent the rest of the week painting benches. He even gave the Dudes one for the dojo.

"I'm gonna enter the good ones in the arts festival, but you can have this one," he said generously.

"It's perfect," said Nate. He mounted it upside down on his mom's old lazy susan and screwed the lazy susan to the top of his camera tripod. After Nate glued foam to the inside of the bench legs, it made a cradle for the Elephant Gun the Dudes had bought at the school auction.

In case you didn't know: years ago the Elephant Gun had been discontinued for being too powerful. So Nate stapled a piece of his mom's exercise strap to the back end of the gun mount to help manage kick-back. Now Ryan wouldn't have to brace himself against Connor when he fired anymore, and no one would get knocked out of the treehouse either.

When the gun mount was finished, it could rotate 360 degrees.

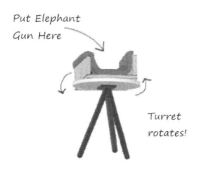

Unfortunately, when Deven took his first shot at an enemy fighter crow, he rotated too far. The foam dart fell short of the bird and landed on the roof of the shed.

Normally, we could have used our zip-line to fly from the top platform of the treehouse to the shed and retrieve the dart. But Dad had recently disconnected the zip-line (after about the third time Connor had slammed into the wall of his office while he was working inside).

Without the zip-line, the Dudes needed another idea.

"I can probably knock it down with a rock," said Connor.

"You can't throw rocks at Dad's office!" I said.

"Right," said Ryan. "We don't want to damage the dart."

It was true. There were only three of the special jumbo darts that had come with the Elephant Gun, so we couldn't afford to ruin one.

"What the Dudes need is a helicopter," said Nate, (not for the first time).

"Or some really bouncy shoes!" suggested Deven.

We talked around a way of trying to use Teresa's trampoline but couldn't figure out how to move it close enough to the shed.

"Maybe we'll get lucky and the wind will blow it down," I suggested.

Then Nate had an inspiration. "Let us be ninja warriors," he said, "and summon a storm."

In **Ninja Tempest** videos, when the ninjas work together to focus their energies they can control the weather. Nate had something like that in mind. He picked up the hose that Grandad had been using to fill Leon's pool and turned on the water.

"If I narrow the spray," said Nate, putting his thumb over the end of the hose, "I can increase the water's velocity."

The water arced up and over the peak of the shed roof before splashing down toward the foam dart.

It was working! The dart began to wiggle and then gently slide downslope.

Nate followed it with the stream of water.

Unfortunately, Dad chose that moment to come out of his office, coffee cup in hand.

"Is it raining?" he asked, squinting across the sunny yard in confusion as water splattered his hair and shoulders.

Just then, Nate managed to nudge the dart off the roof and it landed point down in Dad's mug.

"Good catch, Mr. Reynolds!" shouted Ryan encouragingly.

"Thanks, Dad," I said, walking up to pluck the dart out of the cup. "You can get your coffee now."

"Nevermind," he said, turning back to the shed. "Maybe I've had too much coffee."

I turned off the water, and we all climbed back to the top platform of the treehouse.

"My turn to shoot," I said, drying the dart on my shirt tail before loading it in the Elephant Gun's barrel.

"Point it away from the shed," Nate suggested. So I aimed it toward a much more logical target: Teresa's house. Mrs. Kostenko lives next door to me, and Teresa lives right behind her. So I sent the dart caddy-corner from the Dojo. Unfortunately, the dart hit a tree limb and fell onto the roof of Mrs. Kostenko's gazebo.

"Uh!" said Ryan, slapping his forehead. "Another roof!"

"Tyler's hose won't be long enough to reach this time," Nate predicted.

"Don't worry. I can get it," Connor assured us.

While Connor climbed Mrs. Kostenko's cedar tree and sidestepped out along a fat limb, Ryan patted the Elephant gun, saying, "This thing has power. Can you imagine if we had this gun in *Ninja Tempest III: Battle Season*? We'd dominate level seven when the Samurai Ram knocks down the temple gates."

"I wish Sherwood Heights had a gate," said Deven. "We could totally defend it."

"Against whom?" I asked, "Country Club Highlands?"

"That's the real problem," said Nate, watching Connor hang from his knees to reach the dart. "We lack a satisfying enemy at whom to shoot."

"Like Hotdog Boy," said Deven.

"We could fight your little brother and his friends," said Ryan, remembering Jayden's birthday party when we played capture the flag with five kindergarteners and a teddy bear. "They were pretty tough."

"Nah," I said. "Mom gets mad when I make war on Jayden." I didn't mention that the kindergarteners had won that game—or that we hadn't managed to make a decent shot yet today.

Connor came back with the dart, and we tried again.

"Watch this," said Ryan, taking charge of the gun. He squeezed one eye shut, using the molded plastic sights on the top of the rifle to perfect his aim. "If Teresa were out on her patio right now, I could land this right in her lemonade," he said.

Ryan pulled the trigger, the gun jerked against the exercise strap, and the dart flew diagonally over the fence, across Teresa's yard, and over the lounge chair on Teresa's patio. We heard a distant thump as the dart bounced off the sliding glass door.

Ryan smiled.

"Go get it, Connor," he ordered casually.

"You go get it," rebelled Connor.

"You got Tyler's bullet," Ryan pointed out.

"That was Tyler, this is you," Connor argued.

"Uh, guys," Nate broke in. "Do you hear something?"

When the twins fell silent, I could hear it too. It was a jingling sound…a familiar jingling sound.

As we watched, Teresa's Chihuahua, Teacup, came trotting around from the front yard, spied the elephant dart on the patio, picked it up in his teeth and carried it back around the side of the house and out of sight!

# 5 Dudes Dart Down

Ryan grabbed the Elephant Gun before Connor could cock it again.

"Don't shoot another dart," he said. "We've only got two left!"

"Good thinking," said Nate. He took the two remaining darts and put them in the freezer. The Dudes' mini fridge wasn't plugged in (the Dudes are all about preventing global warming), but it was the closest thing we had to a safe in the dojo.

Then we all swung out of the treehouse like action heroes and ran out of my yard and around the block to Teresa's house.

When we got there, the tiny terror came trotting out of his doggy door to bark at Ryan, but he didn't bring the dart with him.

"It must be in the house," said Connor.

There was only one thing to do. The Dudes clomped up onto the porch, braving Teacup's bulging eyes and needle-sharp teeth to ring the doorbell.

"No one's home, boys," called a voice behind us as a pick-up truck pulled into the drive. *Lopez Construction* was painted on the side along with an artistic sunrise behind a silhouette of a house. This must be Teresa's Uncle Miguel, who built her treehouse and put up the new playground at Sherwood Elementary.

"What do you boys want?" asked Uncle Miguel, getting out of the truck.

"Uh, we were just looking for Teresa," said Ryan.

Uncle Miguel lifted an eyebrow. "I didn't know *mi sobrina* was so popular," he said, joining us on the porch. "I'm afraid she's on vacation."

As he turned to unlock the door, Ryan asked, "Where did she go?"

"They went to Boston," Uncle Miguel explained. "My sister always likes to go somewhere educational on vacation."

(Isn't that just like a principal? No wonder Teresa is the way she is.)

"Uh, how long until she'll be back?" Ryan asked over Teacup's snarling.

I could tell he was making conversation as an excuse to stay on the porch. Maybe the dart would turn out to be close to the door where one of us could grab it.

"They won't be back for a week," said Teresa's Uncle. "I'm just here to feed Teacup."

"Hey, can I help you with that?" offered Ryan cheerfully. "I love dogs!"

Meanwhile, Teacup growled and yapped at Ryan like the mad dog he is.

"Uh, no thanks, boys," said Teresa's uncle. "By the way, you're on camera."

Uncle Miguel pointed toward the corner of the porch ceiling where a small video camera was mounted under the eave.

"My sister had cameras installed all around the house," he explained. "Being a principal makes her a target for pranks, and she likes to know who her enemies are," he said ominously.

Yikes. Middle school was still a whole summer away, but the Dudes already knew we didn't want to get on the bad side of Teresa's mom.

"But we have to get that dart back!" Ryan pointed out when we were safe again in the dojo.

"Maybe we should wait for Teresa to come back and get it for us," I suggested.

"Teacup might have chewed it up by then," Connor said.

"The dart *does* have Ryan's smell on it," Nate pointed out.

"And we all know how Teacup likes to chew on Ryan," agreed Deven.

"Besides, what's Mrs. Gutierrez going to think when she gets back and finds our dart inside her house?" said Ryan.

"We should have asked Teresa's uncle to get the dart for us," said Connor.

"Right," Ryan shot back. "Mr. Lopez, would you please give us the dart we lost when we were shooting at your beloved niece?"

"Teresa wasn't really there," Connor pointed out.

"Sure, we were just *practicing* shooting Teresa," said Ryan. "That would have sounded better."

"But now we'll never get inside," I said.

"Teacup goes in and out all day," Deven observed. "If only we had a Dude that was Teacup size."

That's when Nate spoke up.

"We could use my spy robot!" he said. His eyes were bulging, kinda like Teacup's.

For as long as I've known Nate, he's wanted a remote control spy robot. He had one almost built last spring before the Governor's security guards mistook it for a bomb and drowned it on our school field trip. He must have built a new one since then.

"Perfect!" said Ryan, smoothing the creases on his hat. "We'll call this Operation Robo-Recovery."

So Nate worked on creating a claw arm for his robot and calibrating it to pick up the delicate foam dart without crushing or tearing it. He practiced first with a hot dog and then moved on to a Twinkie.

Connor helped 'cause, you know, Twinkies.

Meanwhile, Deven borrowed his dad's binoculars to scout all sides of the Gutierrez house.

"There are no blind spots big enough for a human to approach unseen," he reported with a salute.

Nate's robot couldn't climb stairs, but Ryan had already figured a way to get the robot onto the porch.

"We can be *seen*," he explained. "We just can't be seen *breaking in*."

An hour later, Connor and Deven went strolling along the sidewalk. As they reached Teresa's house, Deven suddenly shouted, "Oh! Ow! A rock! My shoe! Aggh!"

With Connor's help, Deven hobbled over to Teresa's porch, wailing the whole way. (We had no way of knowing if the cameras recorded sound. For Mrs. Gutierrez's sake, I hoped not.)

Once on the porch steps, Deven made quite a production of removing his shoe and displaying the golf ball-sized rock he had supposedly found there. But all that was cover for Connor, who, screened by Deven's body, removed the robot from his backpack, set it on the porch, and turned it on.

5 Dudes Dart Down

From what we could tell, the cameras were set to cover people from about the waist up, so the robot, at Teacup's height, was safe from being filmed as it rolled smoothly over the porch floorboards and through the doggy door.

A minute later, Deven had a sudden recovery. He and Connor strolled off together, and circled around the block to where the rest of us were hiding behind Teresa's neighbor's hedge.

"I'm turning the robot's camera on so we can see what it sees," Nate said. We all crowded around the screen of his dad's old smartphone which he had converted into a controller for the robot.

The picture was sort of dark, and it jiggled as the robot moved.

"I should have installed a headlight," said Nate regretfully.

Still, we could see hardwood floor stretching away in the distance. Nate steered the robot forward and then around the area rug in the foyer.

"No sense taking chances," he said. "I'm not sure the wheels will work on carpet."

I nodded. The last thing we wanted was for our robot to get stuck in Teresa's house.

Soon we could see cabinets on both sides, and we guessed the robot was passing through the kitchen. In the hall, the robot stopped in front of two dark doorways, the den and a bathroom, before reaching the door at the end.

Teresa's room was toward the back of the house and, luckily, on the ground floor.

The robot maneuvered inside and rotated its body to survey the room.

To one side was Teacup's tiny brass bed covered with fancy pillows and a little stuffed dog. It was an exact replica of Teresa's bed except that Teacup kept his neater—and he had decorated his bed with an elephant dart.

"There it is!" shouted Ryan. "Grab it."

But there was a problem. Nothing moved on the screen. Nate was pushing buttons, but the bed wasn't getting any closer and the claw arm wasn't moving either. We could see the dart, but we couldn't get it!

# 6 Dudes Save the Day

"We're too far away," said Nate. "The robot's wifi receiver can't read the signal!"

The Dudes groaned.

"Okay, okay. Don't despair, Dudes," said Ryan. "We just need a new plan—one that will get Nate close enough to control the robot."

"He can't get close to the house because of the cameras," I pointed out.

"I got it!" said Connor. "We let the cameras record Nate. Then we use the robot to erase the recording like they do on TV."

But Nate had to burst his bubble. "The robot is only designed to go forward, back, turn, and carry a dart," said Nate. "Besides, we don't know where the video is saved. It might be online."

"Yeah," I said, "For all we know, Mrs. Gutierrez is watching her yard right now from Paul Revere's House in Boston."

"The Dudes are coming! The Dudes are coming!" Deven yelled, pretending to ride a horse.

"We're doomed," Connor said. "Teresa will come home and find Nate's robot in her room and Mrs. Guttierrez will expel us before we even start middle school."

"I don't want to give my mom another excuse to homeschool me," said Nate. He'd faced that particular doom before.

"It's okay, Dudes," Ryan reassured us. "We'll get the robot back. We just need to think of an innocent reason to be hanging out in Teresa's yard."

"We could be pulling weeds or something," Deven suggested.

"Like us doing Teresa's chores isn't suspicious," I said.

Ryan shook his head. "We have to do something that isn't so unexpected," he said.

"Teresa's mom is expecting to be pranked," said Connor.

Ryan snapped his fingers, "Then we'll make sure she gets what she's expecting!" he said, and Operation Neighborhood Hero was born.

We went back to my yard where Nate drew a diagram of Teresa's house in Jayden's sandbox.

"I'll need to get close to Teresa's window," said Nate, putting an "X" in the side yard near the gate to the back.

"For how long?" asked Ryan.

"Assuming no interference, it should take no more than two minutes to manipulate the robot claw and then drive the robot to the front of the house," Nate said, mimicking the operation with the smartphone in his hands.

"It looks like he's playing a videogame," Connor said.

"That's innocent!" said Deven.

"Except why would Nate be playing a video game under Teresa's window?" I said. "He's not waiting for a bus."

But Ryan grinned. "He's waiting for *you* to catch the prankster," he said.

"Me?!"

"You live the closest," Ryan explained. "You'd be most likely to notice something suspicious like a bad middle schooler in Teresa's yard."

"I get it!" said Connor. Then he frowned. "Only where do we get a bad middle schooler?"

"One of us will have to play that part," Ryan revealed.

"Me! Me!" pleaded Deven, raising his hand.

Ryan nodded. "Okay. Now, what kind of prank would this bad middle schooler pull?" he asked.

"Ooh! Donuts on the lawn!" Deven suggested. "Dad was really mad when somebody drove circles in our yard last year. It turned out to be some guy who had a crush on my sister," Deven explained. "Shaila broke his heart, and he broke Dad's."

I could see a problem with making tire tracks on Mrs. Gutierrez's lawn. "Middle schoolers can't drive, remember?"

"But this is a *bad* middle schooler," said Deven.

"But *you* can't drive," said Ryan.

"Oh yeah," said Deven, disappointed.

"You'll have to wear a disguise," said Ryan, which perked Deven up again.

"And act furtive," said Nate, "like you don't want to be seen."

"But don't avoid the cameras," put in Ryan. "We want to put on a nice show for Mrs. Gutierrez to distract from what Nate's *really* doing."

Deven snapped to attention. "You can count on me!" he vowed.

"You should carry gear that shows you're up to no good," said Nate.

"Spray paint," I suggested, remembering graffiti I'd seen on the restrooms in the park.

"And toilet paper!" added Connor.

And on that note, we put Operation Neighborhood Hero into action.

First we went over to Deven's house to get his disguise. We had agreed that his face should be covered by Grandad's fishing hat pulled low over his eyes. But it was Deven who had the idea to borrow some foam padding that his grandmother was using to make new cushions for the patio furniture. By the time we'd wrapped foam around his arms, chest, and shoulders, Deven looked like a new man—or rather a husky middle-schooler with a grudge.

Of course, none of his shirts fit.

"Ooh! Dad's got a stretchy one that should work," he said.

When Deven was ready, we walked out through the living room, where Mr. Singh was reading the set-up instructions for a new flat-screen TV. He glanced up, then looked again.

"Is that my new golf shirt?" he asked.

"I'm just borrowing it, Dad," said Deven.

"But…" said Mr. Singh, gesturing vaguely toward his son's new physique.

"Love this high tech performance fabric," said Deven quickly. "Gotta go."

Next we stopped by Nate's house to pick up the TP and spray paint.

"My mom always has art supplies," Nate explained, "and, uh, bathroom supplies."

Then we went back to our temporary headquarters behind the hedge near Teresa's driveway. It's a lucky thing her neighbors work all day and weren't there to interfere with our operation.

According to plan, the bad middle schooler went in first. Carrying a shopping bag in one hand and three rolls of toilet paper on a stick in the other, he crossed the front yard furtively. When he reached the end of the porch, he set down his shopping bag and took out a can of spray paint.

That was my cue. Nate and I emerged from behind the bush and strolled innocently past on the sidewalk.

We were chatting amiably when Deven started shaking the paint can, making that little ball inside rattle.

Nate and I stopped, reacting like we could hear something (well, of course, we *could* hear it). We looked all around for the source of the noise.

"Hey!" I yelled as Nate pointed dramatically to the "villain" in Teresa's side yard.

"What are you doing? Get away from there!" I shouted as Nate and I started toward the spot.

Seeing us, the bad guy dropped his paint can and ran, leaving the shopping bag and slipping through the gate to the back yard before Nate and I could catch him.

When we reached Teresa's window, I held Nate back and shouted, "You stay here, and keep watch!"

"Okay!" shouted Nate, nodding emphatically. He leaned against the house and took out his smartphone.

When I reached the back yard, I could see Deven having a great time T-P-ing Teresa's treehouse and trampoline, throwing the rolls high in the trees, where the paper would catch in the branches and unroll on the way down.

"Unhand that toilet paper!" I shouted. (That's something I never thought I'd hear myself say.)

Deven whirled, spotted me, jumped comically high in the air, then took off running around the other side of the house, out of Teresa's yard and up the street, the stick with two toilet paper rolls still clutched in his right hand.

I too, ran out of the yard as if to chase him. I was supposed to wait behind the hedge, then come back, huffing and puffing, to collect Nate. But there was a problem.

Luckily, the remote control was also a phone. Nate dialed Deven's number and Deven put it on speaker so all of us behind the hedge could hear.

"The operation of the claw was successful," Nate reported in hushed tones. "However, there was a variable we failed to consider in our plan."

"What?" said Ryan.

"Teacup," Nate answered.

"He's attacking the robot?" I asked. If the little dog knocked the robot off its wheels we'd never get it out of there.

"Not...attacking," Nate replied hesitantly.

It seems that all that practicing with hot dogs and Twinkies made the robot smell tasty. And, besides that, it was now holding Teacup's favorite toy. Nate couldn't tell if Teacup was trying to make friends with the robot or eat it, but he could see a lot of the Chihuahua's nose, teeth and tongue on the monitor.

I shuddered.

"I need more time to complete the extraction," whispered Nate, "and some way to get past Teacup. I wish I had equipped the robot with a laser blaster."

"Don't worry about Teacup," Ryan told Nate. "Just be ready to get that robot out of there."

Then he switched hats with Deven. "Give me your muscles," Ryan said. "I'm going in!"

I wasn't sure it would work.

But, when Ryan ran onto the sidewalk in front of Teresa's house and yelled: "I'm back, little dog. Come and get me!" Teacup came tearing out the doggy door, snarling and yipping, causing Ryan to wish the padding was on the bottom half of his body.

"Better hurry up, Nate," Deven said into the phone, "or Ryan's gonna be kibble."

Nate slowly returned to the front yard, his eyes never leaving his "video game" as he guided the robot, with its precious foam cargo, out the doggie door and off the side of the porch, right into the shopping bag the "bad middle schooler" had left there.

"Mission accomplished," said Nate quietly.

Deven gave the signal, and Ryan lunged for the neighbor's yard, causing Teacup to unclench his jaws from Ryan's pants leg before he could be dragged over the invisible fence and get a zap from his collar.

Meanwhile, I returned from my "search for the bad guy" and picked up the shopping bag.

"We'd better take this as evidence," I said loudly. Then Nate and I casually walked off into the sunset.

One day, about a week later, Teresa came into her back yard and called toward the dojo across the back fence.

"Hi Teresa," said Ryan coolly. "Did you have a good vacation?"

"Of course," answered Teresa. "But I think you had more excitement here at home. Luckily, we have a new security system that caught everything on video," she said proudly. "Come see."

The Dudes looked at each other. Did she know?

"I'm eager to see how our fabrication turned out," Nate said as we walked around the corner to Teresa's house.

"You realize, of course, she might be calling us over there to make things easier for the police," I pointed out.

"Or worse, her mom!" said Deven.

Teresa greeted us at the door with Teacup in her arms. She led us into her den and tapped the screen of a tablet. The TV came to life with a screen split to show the recordings from four different cameras.

It turns out there was no sound, which made it kind of like watching one of those old-fashioned silent movies. I could hear the leather sofas creaking under us as we nervously watched the story play out.

When it was done, I could breathe a little easier. It didn't look like we'd made any mistakes, and the robot had never appeared on video.

Teresa paused on a shot of Deven in disguise.

"You chased him, Tyler," she said. "Do you have any idea who this guy is? He seems familiar."

"Um, he looks tough," I said vaguely.

"Yeah, a big guy!" said Deven, sinking down in his seat.

"It was nice of you to chase him," Teresa said as she cuddled Teacup. "But Nate wasn't much help. He never took his eyes off his phone. What game were you playing anyway?" she asked suddenly.

"Uh," said Nate, blinking in surprise.

"It was Manic Manic Meatball Meatball," I said, jumping in with the first thing I could think of.

"It's addictive," added Nate.

"Oh," said Teresa. "Well, anyway, I guess it's good to know we have a real hero in the neighborhood."

My ears started to burn the way they always do when I'm embarrassed. But then she added, "When that bad guy eluded Tyler, *Teacup* really saved the day!"

7 Dudes Make a Splash

After the zip-tie incident, Mr. Maguire decided it was a good idea for the twins to spend less time at home in their garage. Luckily, the Sherwood Parks Department has a lot of fun ways to keep your kids supervised in the summer. Ryan and Connor signed up to spend afternoons in July playing in the Summer Fun Baseball League.

At the first game, the coach of the Sherwood Sharks told the team that winning didn't matter. And I guess he was serious about that because he made Connor the pitcher and Ryan the catcher for the first game.

In the first inning, Connor ignored Ryan's signals and pitched whatever he wanted. So Ryan gave Connor a piece of his mind—and his fist—in the dugout which resulted in the coach putting them at opposite ends of the bench.

In the second inning, Connor pitched the *opposite* of whatever Ryan signaled. And, when they got to the dugout, he took off his shoe and threw it at Ryan. Which resulted in the first baseman using an ice pack and everyone else on the team putting on their batting helmets.

In the third inning, Ryan signaled an intentional walk but Connor threw his patented spinning curve ball instead. The hitter whacked the ball and ran toward first base. Meanwhile, Ryan ran toward the mound where he proceeded to tackle the pitcher.

That started a knock-down-drag-out on the field with the rest of the Sherwood team taking sides and the runner and the whole opposing team looking on in confusion.

The umpire wasn't confused, though. He threw the Sherwood team out of the game for unsportsmanlike conduct and gave the win to the Nottingham Cougars.

I guess that's when the coach decided that winning mattered after all. He threw Ryan and Connor off the team. Which is why, after the first week of July, Ryan and Connor were free to spend more time at my house.

Nate and Deven were there too. Deven was hiding out to avoid having to practice piano. And Nate was there because he didn't know what else to do with his free time, never having had any. You see, Nate's summers had always been filled with what his mom called "enrichment activities" like Rocket Workshop and Latin Camp. But, this year, his mom said she was giving him "time for the fermentation of his creativity."

"What's fertemnation?" asked Deven.

"Fermentation basically means rotting," Nate explained, "and usually involves the production of gas and heat."

"I'm pretty sure your mom's expecting something else," I pointed out.

"You're right," said Nate glumly. "She convinced the Sherwood Arts Committee to add a Young Filmmakers contest to the Arts Festival this year," he told us. "I'm supposed to be using my free time to produce a film worthy of entering."

Ryan shrugged. "No problem," he said. "Your zombie video was awesome."

It was true. The zombie apocalypse video we'd made last summer was still getting lots of views online.

Nate nodded. "That's what gave her the idea," he said. "But my new video won't be judged by people who like cool videos," he pointed out, "just experts. Besides, I'm not sure I can produce under pressure."

"Are you kidding?" said Ryan. "That's what Dudes do."

"Lately, my mind has been occupied with a more practical project," Nate confessed.

"What's that?" I asked.

"I'm fitting my spy robot with tank tracks," Nate answered.

"You can't get more practical than that," said Ryan seriously.

About that time, Grandad came out of the house and started strapping Leon into his stroller.

"There's a big to-do over at the park this afternoon," Grandad told us. "I read about it in the Sherwood Spotlight."

(Grandad reads the Sherwood Spotlight web feed every day. He calls it "keeping an eye on the mayor".)

"A lot of construction going on in Sherwood--a lot of money being spent, a lot of *changes*," Grandad went on.

"You say that like it's a bad thing," I said.

"We won't know 'til we check it out for ourselves," said Granddad, taking firm hold of the handlebar so Jayden couldn't dump the baby out. "If we walk while Leon takes his nap, we'll be there for free punch and cookies."

Punch and cookies are just about the only things that could have enticed Jayden into walking all the way down the hill to Sherwood Downtown Park, but he still shot evil looks at Leon for getting the stroller.

The Dudes just happened to be free that afternoon, so we decided to come along.

Sherwood Downtown Park had been fenced off and under construction for almost a whole year. They were replacing the old, graffiti-covered restrooms and adding a playground and splash park for little kids with a wall around it so the kids can't get away from their keepers. On the other side of the wall, would be a new skate park for teens. Unfortunately, that wasn't opening until the end of the summer. The rest of the park would have trees and nature and stuff, which, I guess, covered the needs of old folks.

On the way we passed a lot with a sign for "Valley View Estates—Coming Soon!"

Grandad shook his head.

"I remember when that was a farm," he complained. "Tear down the old, build up the new. That's the idea these days. New parks, new apartments, new houses…"

The Dudes looked at each other and shrugged. Adults don't always make a lot of sense.

When we got to the park, the mayor was making a speech. I guess she wanted to take credit for spending Grandad's money before cutting the big blue ribbon that stretched across the entry gate.

"I wonder where she gets those giant scissors," Ryan whispered.

The mayor said the new playground had all the latest features. So right away I was thinking public trampolines or maybe virtual reality.

But it turned out she was talking about energy efficiency and recycled materials. The water in the splash park was recycled too. I figured that would please Grandad in case he liked his water old, like his houses.

"This new park is just another example of how the city of Sherwood is preparing for the future!" the mayor announced.

It was a hot day, and the mayor, in her red hat, stood like a big flower in the shade of some artificial palm trees that formed the entry to the park. When she finally cut the ribbon, kids ran screaming toward the play area.

The Dudes ran toward the refreshment table instead, that's how we ran into a reporter who was asking people what they thought of the park.

Reactions to the new restrooms were mixed. Moms liked the padded diaper changing stations. Little kids disliked the loud automatic flushes. But everybody was glad the graffiti-covered walls had been replaced by stylish pink brick.

"How do you feel about the new family-style restrooms?" the reporter asked Connor. (He meant they are the kind where the whole family can go in together instead of separate boys' and girls' rooms.)

Connor took a swig of punch to wash down the four cookies in his mouth. Then he said, "Uh, I guess I'm glad that moms will stop asking me to go in the men's room to drag out little boys that are playing in the sink."

The reporter raised his eyebrows. I think it was a side of the restroom issue he hadn't heard before. Of course, there was no need to play in the sink now that Sherwood had a splash park. Speaking of which, we decided to head over there.

By the gate, Grandpa had cornered the mayor to ask about the city's Emergency Preparedness Budget.

"I'm not ready to reveal my plans, yet," the mayor said mysteriously. "But rest assured, the town of Sherwood will be ready for any emergency."

"I bet she's building a secret weapon," said Ryan, straightening his hat. "That's what I'd do."

"My mother joined the emergency preparedness committee at the middle school," Nate said. "She says it's mostly about stocking up on hand sanitizer."

"I bet the mayor has got a secret bunker *full* of hand sanitizer," said Connor, "like the president."

"And Batman," Jayden added, pulling at Grandad's arm.

Leon woke up just then and started spouting word pieces, so Grandad steered him away from the mayor and followed us through the gate.

When he saw the splash park, Jayden shrieked, flung off his shoes and socks, and ran into the spray.

"Well, boys," said Grandad, rescuing Jayden's sock before Leon could put it in his mouth. "What do you think?"

"Not bad," said Ryan, putting his hands in his pockets.

"It's okay," said Connor, rolling his shoulders the way his dad does.

"It's good for little kids," I said, playing it cool.

"It's not like sixth-graders want to frolic in the sprinklers," added Nate.

Of course, just then, Deven came zig-zagging across the park with his shoes off and his arms in the air.

The splash park had a nautical theme with boats and sea animals. The "beach" and "rocks" and "palm trees" were all made out of rubbery foam that was easy to walk and climb on and wouldn't smash you up too bad if you fell on your head. Water sprang into the air from jets all over the area. There was even a big orca squirting water from his spout while kids climbed his tail and slid down his nose.

"Isn't a beached whale supposed to be a bad thing?" I said. But this one looked happy, smiling wide so kids could climb over his rubbery teeth.

Meanwhile, Deven was using his older-kid knowledge to elevate the experience for everyone.

"Look," he said, pushing his thumb into one of the jets. "If you narrow the spray you can increase the water's velosoapy!" he said, directing the spray toward a nearby rocking boat.

Shrill screams rose from the vessel, and the girl in the front seat turned her sprinkler on Deven.

In no time, Deven had started a trend and every jet had some little kid hovering over it, trying to direct the water with his hand or his foot or some other body part.

"Let's water the plants," said one girl.

A group of kids knelt and pushed their hands into the spray, directing it up to the top of the rubbery palm fronds at the gate.

The mayor was still beneath the palms, snagging voters for handshakes and pictures with her big scissors. Luckily, the cupped leaves collected the falling water.

Meanwhile, Deven was having a water battle with the kid on top of the whale.

I saw the kid's spray hit Deven in the face.

"Avast, you devil dog!" Deven cried, possibly reliving his trauma on the *S.S. Dudes* as he returned fire.

Deven wasn't the only one who went home wet that day.

The <u>Sherwood Spotlight</u> had a picture of the mayor smiling with a gallon of water hanging above her hat in the instant before the palm frond finally dipped and drenched her.

The caption read: *Is Mayor Prepared for What's Coming?* And the story was all about questions surrounding the emergency preparedness budget.

Grandad laughed. "That photographer was lucky to be in the right place at the right time," he said.

But, of course, he had a little help from Deven.

8 Dudes Shake It Up

It was a warm day when Ryan and Connor and I went over to Deven's house to pick him up on the way to Nate's. When we got there, we could hear loud piano sounds (I wouldn't call it music) coming through the open windows of the living room.

The guys and I hesitated on the sidewalk.

"Maybe we shouldn't disturb his practice," I said.

Connor winced. "It sounds like he needs it," he agreed.

But, just then, we saw Deven strolling toward us up the driveway.

"Huh?" said Connor.

"Who's practicing the piano?" Ryan asked. "That's not your sister."

Deven grinned. "No way," he assured us. "Shaila's allergic to mistakes. She puts earplugs in when I practice." He wiggled his eyebrows and added, "which is why she'll never notice I recorded *yesterday's practice* to play on repeat."

The Dudes were high-fiving Deven when we suddenly heard Mr. Singh's stern voice coming through the screens on the upstairs windows.

"Deven!" he shouted. "You must stop practicing now. Do you hear me, son?" he called, his voice sounding loud then soft then loud again as he left the bedroom and marched downstairs toward the living room. "Deven! I can't hear myself think!"

"Uh-oh!" said Deven. "I forgot it was Dad's day off. Let's get out of here, Dudes!" Deven sprinted down the sidewalk, and the rest of us followed him. Nobody wanted to be around when Mr. Singh discovered Deven's phone on the piano bench.

At Nate's house, Mrs. Howe ushered us through the front door with a smile, so I guess she figured we were there to help Nate with his video production. Ever since we made that zombie video last summer, she had learned to accept that the Dudes were part of Nate's creative process.

"I'm having a meeting of the Emergency Preparedness Committee for the middle school today," Mrs. Howe explained, "but I'm sure we won't disturb your work."

I was pretty sure too, since Nate didn't have any ideas yet.

The doorbell rang again, and Mrs. Howe went to answer it.

"Refreshments!" said Connor, spotting a table with little sandwiches and pink cookies.

The Dudes surrounded it and attacked.

"Better eat something, Deven," said Ryan, "this may be your last meal."

"Don't worry," Deven answered. "Shaila's the one who will get it for not supervising my practice."

We were laughing with our mouths full when a shadow fell over us. We turned and found ourselves face to face with Teresa's mother.

"It's nice to see you, boys," said Mrs. Guttierrez in that way she had of sounding like she was glad to see you so she can keep an eye on you.

The Dudes swallowed.

"Hi, Mrs. Guttierrez," said Ryan, suddenly remembering to take off his hat in the house.

"Teresa, don't you want to say hello to your friends?" asked her mother.

I hadn't noticed Teresa there. But then, her mother did sort of fill up a room. I don't mean she's fat, it's just that she's conspicuous, like a battleship in a small harbor, or a middle school principal in a small living room.

"Hello, boys," said Teresa, as she took a seat on the sofa beside her mother.

Teresa always called us "boys" like we were all one person, or interchangeable even. She almost never called us by our names unless she was accusing one of us of something: "Connor Maguire is doing water fountain stunts in the hall! Tyler Reynolds is reading The Three Musketeers instead of social studies! Deven Singh is imitating my hairstyle!"

Mrs. Howe returned to the living room with three other mothers—not our own, thank goodness. She frowned when she saw what was left of the refreshments.

The grown-ups started introducing themselves and shaking hands.

"I'll call Nate," Mrs. Howe offered. She pushed a button that was taped to the wall above the light switch and spoke into a little mesh panel.

There was a similar set-up in Nate's room. It was an intercom system he had built out of old toy walkie-talkies—just one of Nate's many projects to provide better living through technology…and duct tape. Since his parents thought everything he did was genius, they didn't mind him taping up their walls.

In a moment, Nate came down the stairs from his bedroom.

Meanwhile, Mrs. Howe was explaining that the job of the committee was to collect and count supplies. They would be kept in a big storage container which would sit at the far edge of the middle school grounds. (That way, I guess, if the school building falls down in some disaster, the hand sanitizer will be safe to clean the hands of those who manage to crawl across the soccer field.)

I could tell right away that middle school was going to be different. The only emergencies we had in elementary school had been the ones Connor created with his water fountain stunts.

"The mayor's office has provided these pamphlets to help us plan what supplies we'll need for each emergency," explained Mrs. Howe.

I looked at the artful array of pamphlets on the coffee table and wondered if that was how the mayor had spent the emergency budget. If so, she did the right thing. It was obvious there was no emergency situation you couldn't solve with the right pamphlet.

The Dudes perused the smorgasbord of emergencies. The earthquake pamphlet immediately caught my eye. It showed a man's silhouette teetering on the edge of a giant crack that had just opened in the ground under him.

That's the kind of thing you can't help hoping might happen someday just so you'd get the chance to see it in real life.

I showed it to Ryan.

"Cool!" he said.

Mrs. Howe frowned. "Perhaps the young people would like to relax in the comfort of Nate's room," she suggested.

Mrs. Howe often called us young people. Like a lot of adults, I think she was hoping that, if she didn't say it, we wouldn't know we were kids. Right away, she started acting like we had already left and began to move around the room with a tray of coffee and creamer.

The Dudes shrugged, figuring the comfort of Nate's room sounded pretty good—especially since Teresa was staying with the adults. (Of course, we hit the refreshment table again, while it was unguarded.)

"What are you here for anyway, Teresa?" Ryan asked, putting a couple extra sandwiches in his hat.

"I'm here because I'm interested," Teresa answered. "An emergency could happen any time, and we spend most of our time at school. Think about it. Don't you want the school to be prepared in case of emergency?"

"I agree with my daughter," said Mrs. Guttierrez, who (surprise!) was listening in to the "young people" conversation the whole time. Sneaky.

Teresa swelled up, making Troy Diamond's face on her T-shirt look like he had a mouth full of marshmallows.

Then Mrs. Guttierrez added, "I think the boys should stay too."

Troy Diamond's face stayed fat, but now Teresa's mouth twisted like her lemonade was unsweetened.

"Perhaps young people should be involved in this process," said her mother to the group of nodding parents. "In my experience, students don't take our emergency drills as seriously as they should."

(*Because they're lame*, I added silently.)

"The drills are lame, Mom," said Teresa.

Whoa! Not only was she right, but I had never heard anybody talk that way to Mrs. Guttierrez. Even her neighbor, Mrs. Kostenko was careful not to get on her bad side ever since the great rain barrel debate.

"I *like* the earthquake drills," said Deven. "Going under the tables is a good way to find loose change and other lost stuff."

"Fire drills are better," Ryan argued. "We get to go outside, and we miss more class time."

"That's time we could be learning," said Teresa.

"My point exactly," said Ryan.

"Besides that," Connor pointed out, "if the school were really burning down, we'd have a great view!"

Mrs. Guttierrez had remained quiet while we were hashing out the issues, but now she said, "If it was really happening, you'd need to know what to do. A fire or an earthquake is no joke."

"The problem is the drill doesn't seem real," said Teresa, crossing her arms over Troy Diamond's nose. "Anybody can crawl under a table when nothing's happening. You don't get to practice the shaking part."

"You're right, Teresa!" said Deven. "But I have a solution: We should hook each kid up to your dad's paint-mixing machine!" Then he demonstrated what that would be like.

Unfortunately, he was holding a platter of cookies at the time.

Pink disks flew around the room like a girly alien invasion! Dudes batted cookies away from their faces.

Mothers lunged to shield their coffees. Mrs. Howe took cover under the breakfast bar.

"That's enough, Mr. Singh!" said Teresa's mom in her principal voice, causing Deven to stop shaking…and the rest of us to start.

9 Dude Quake

Mrs. Guttierrez stood up, brushing crumbs off her pants but missing the ones on her hair and shoulders. It looked like she had pink dandruff.

"Uh, time to go, Dev," said Nate, pushing Deven toward the hall before Teresa could finish dusting off her mom. The rest of us Dudes followed up the stairs.

When we reached Nate's room, he punched in a code on the keypad taped to his door. But, when he opened the door, we all shuddered at the cacophony caused by the music of seventeen solar powered dancing monkeys activated at once.

"Ooh! They're playing my song!" said Deven, dancing while the rest of us held our ears.

"Oops!" shouted Nate over the din. "I forgot I changed the code."

He rushed across the room, pulled the shade, and reset the hook that held it down.

The racket stopped.

"Something tells me we're safe from Teresa," I said over the ringing in my head.

Nate nodded, closing the door behind us. "The monkey music is an effective deterrent," he confirmed. "However, they require me to keep the room dark," he added.

"Teresa was right about the earthquake drills, though," Connor said. "If we had a real quake we wouldn't be ready."

Ryan nodded. "There's gotta be a better way to practice what to do in an earthquake," he complained. "I mean, nothing's falling, nobody's screaming."

"It does not accurately represent the true circumstances of an emergency," Nate agreed.

Luckily, I was still holding the earthquake pamphlet. I opened it, leaned in close to Nate's Tardis nightlight and read: *"Plan how you would drop, cover, and hold on until the shaking stopped."*

The picture showed a man on his hands and knees under a table, holding onto its legs. This raised some questions from all of us:

Ryan: "What if you don't have a table?"

Me: "What if your little brother is already *under* the table?"

Nate: "What if you're in a restaurant and the floor is gross?"

Connor: "What if you're outside in a tree?"

Deven: "What if one of those cracks opens up and swallows your piano?"

We decided to watch some videos online to see what real earthquakes were like. (I know what Mr. Maguire said, but this was practically a school assignment. Even my mom allows screen time for schoolwork.)

Nate found that there were lots of videos available, including an old movie that showed giant lava-hot cockroaches coming out of a crack in the earth. (Bad news for the silhouette man on the pamphlet!)

Another video claimed to be of the earthquake that swallowed the lost continent of Atlantis, but it looked like it was filmed in someone's dirty bathtub.

Finally Nate found videos posted by real earthquake survivors in Japan.

From these videos we learned that the actual experience of an earthquake was not much like either the school earthquake drills or the situation presented in the pamphlet. For instance, the pamphlet said not to stand in a doorway. But a lot of people in the videos were standing in doorways. They were probably being filmed by the people who had beat them out for space under the table.

I don't know if they have pamphlets in Japan, but it looked like the plan to "drop, cover, and hold" hadn't caught on. There were people in a grocery store who ran around screaming while others tried to continue shopping. There were people who tried to balance like they were riding the waves on a surf board and others who sat down, turned the camera on themselves, and made insightful blog entries.

"You think it's really possible to do all that while the ground is shaking?" I asked.

"Dudes, we gotta find out!" said Ryan. "Nate, can you cause an earthquake?"

Luckily for Sherwood Heights, he couldn't.

"It would be easier to create an earthquake simulator," said Nate thoughtfully. "Such mechanisms are used to test building designs under disaster conditions." He put on his green protective goggles and said, "Let's go to Tyler's house."

9 Dude Quake

So the Dudes slipped past the Emergency Preparedness Committee. They were now talking about something called "space blankets" which sounded cool. But I was busy worrying that testing my house under earthquake conditions was liable to test my mom to the breaking point.

Luckily, it turned out Nate wanted to use the *treehouse*. As you may remember, the treehouse dojo the Dudes built last summer consisted of three separate wooden platforms which aren't cluttered up by anything like roofs or walls. We took the tent off of one of them, and, as it turned out, un-nailing it from the tree was super easy too.

Meanwhile, Ryan and Connor went home and walked back rolling their Dad's and Tina's inner tubes, which Mr. Maguire was storing in the garage. We stacked the tubes on top of one another and set the platform on top of that.

I used Grandad's drill to make holes in the corners of the platform. Then Nate tied on the ropes from the zip-line and ran them through pulleys over our heads. (It was a lucky thing Dad had a meeting downtown today, so there was nobody to yell at us for all the noise we made anchoring the pulleys to the shed.)

Four of us stood at the corners of the platform. When we heaved on the ropes, the platform dipped and shimmied crazily on top of the inner tubes.

"Okay," said Ryan. "We have to practice Drop, Cover, and Hold."

The platform wasn't big enough for a full-size table, so I brought out the kid-size table and chair Grandad had made for Jayden.

Nate recorded a flash drive with the sounds of an earthshaking rumble too. "For verisimilitude," he said, as he pulled a portable speaker out of his backpack.

"Huh?" said Deven.

"I mean it will be like the real thing," Nate explained. He plugged the flash drive in the speaker and set up his video

9 Dude Quake

recorder on a tripod to capture the action. Now all we needed was a guinea pig.

"Ooh! Me! Me!" shouted Deven. Then he ran inside, yelling, "Just a second! I need props!"

He returned with a plate of plastic food and a plastic tea cup and saucer from the basement play kitchen. He was also wearing his Random Noise wig and a fake mustache. He climbed up onto the platform and sat down in the chair.

"I believe I'll have a spot of tea," he said, all unsuspecting, as he raised his cup with his pinkie extended.

Ryan gave the signal, and we started yanking on the ropes. The platform shook. The dull rumble from the speaker rose to a roar. And Deven began to bounce in his seat.

His mustache flew off his face like a hairy butterfly. The rubber cupcake launched off the plate and bounced against the shed window. Water sloshed out of the cup into his face.

"Tsunami!" Deven yelled. Blinking, he reached out to feel for the table, which was scooting across the vibrating platform.

"Don't let it get away!" shouted Connor

By the time Deven got his head under the table, it was hanging by two legs, and the chair had fallen on Connor's foot.

When the simulation was over, Deven rolled off the platform and staggered around the yard, wiping his face and slinging the water out of his wig like a dog.

"Maybe we should *try* it with a dog," said Connor. "You think Teresa would let us use precious Teacup?"

"No way," said Ryan. "Get your baby brother, Tyler."

But, just then, the timer on Connor's watch reminded us that Ryan and Connor had to get back to the garage to get supervised by their dad. The rest of the Dudes decided to join them and get supervised too while we ate some warehouse-brand popsicles out of Mrs. Maguire's extra freezer. Earthquake simulations are hot work.

The next morning, we returned to the Dojo for more earthquake action.

Connor was riding the bucking platform this time, and we had hardly started the speakers when Dad came rushing out of his office.

9 Dude Quake

"Sorry, Dad," I said. "You were so quiet, we didn't know you were here!"

"What is going on out here?" he demanded.

"It's only an earthquake, Mr. Reynolds," Ryan explained.

"We are creating a simulation to aid in emergency preparedness," Nate clarified.

"It feels like there's a freight train coming through," Dad complained.

"That's versimillipede," Deven explained proudly.

"The simulation is not actually complete," Nate pointed out, turning off the speaker. "In a real earthquake Connor would be in danger from falling objects."

"I could throw bricks at him," Ryan suggested.

"No!" roared Dad.

Then he tried to calm down, which, by the way, *is* the proper procedure during an emergency. It's in the pamphlet.

"Boys," he said. "I'm very busy. Whatever this is...you'll have to stop for today."

"Awww!" moaned Deven. "I wanted to try it with pudding."

"Whatever you say, Mr. Reynolds," said Ryan agreeably.

And Nate said, "Perhaps we should try soil liquefaction now."

Dad's eyes kind of bounced around his head. Then he took another deep breath and said, "As long as you don't do it here."

"Sure," said Ryan. "Okay, guys. The earthquake is over."

It was funny, though, because, when Dad went back in his office, he was still shaking.

 ## *10 Dudes Prepared*

That night, we were eating sloppy joes at dinner. Well, Mom and Dad and Jayden and I were. Leon was eating his usual mush—we'll call it 'sloppy Leon'.

Mom said, "The fire alarm went off at work today."

"A drill?" asked Dad.

"That's what I thought," said Mom, "but then the fire trucks rolled up. It turned out some appliance had shorted out in the cafeteria and caused an electrical fire."

"That's why I'm glad I work at home," said Dad, taking a satisfied bite of his joe.

"Did you see the fire, Mom?" I asked.

"No," she answered. "They kept us outside for an hour. But lots of people hadn't thought it was real and didn't even leave the building!" she said, outraged.

"Yeah, I hate those interruptions," Dad commented absentmindedly.

Mom frowned. "It made me think about what *we* would do in an emergency," she said. "I think we should have a fire drill."

Mom stared until Dad looked up from his plate.

"Now?" he asked.

Mom's frown didn't move.

"Right," said Dad. "No time like the present."

"There's gonna be presents?" asked my little brother.

"No, Jayden," I said. "There's gonna be noise."

Mom took her kitchen chair to the hallway, stood on it and pushed the test button on the fire alarm until it gave an ear-piercing shriek.

So did Leon. And *he* didn't stop when Mom let go of the button.

"I got him," shouted Dad, prying the screaming baby out of his highchair and hugging sloppy Leon to his chest.

Jayden began to wail too, "Mom, Mom, Mom, Mom, Mom!" as he clung to her leg.

"We've got to go outside!" Mom and Dad yelled as they passed each other with fingers in their ears. Then Mom pried Jayden's hands from around her leg and started dragging him toward the deck door. Meanwhile, Dad elbowed open the garage door and carried Leon out that way.

The kitchen fell silent. I thought seriously about hanging out to see if they even missed me. But I figured, in a real emergency, it wouldn't be safe to leave the rest of my family to deal with it on their own.

Still, just to be different, I went out the front door.

The yard was not exactly peaceful.

"Jason?" yelled Mom's voice from the backyard.

"Meg?" called Dad from the side yard.

"Mom, Mom, Mom, Mom!" wailed Jayden.

Eventually we found each other.

"I think that went pretty well," said Dad as we gathered in the driveway. "I guess we can go back inside now."

"Wait," said Mom. "We got separated this time. We should probably choose a safe meeting place."

(In case there happens to be heavy fog on the night our house catches fire, I guess.)

Mom looked around. "The sidewalk, maybe," she suggested. "That should be far enough from the house."

We moved three steps onto the sidewalk. Yep, this was keeping us totally safe.

But Jayden expressed a lack of confidence in the plan. "I don't want to have a fire," he said.

"We're not going to *have* a fire," said Dad wincing as Leon amused himself by pushing slop into Dad's ear.

"Then why are we having a fire drill?" Jayden asked, his lip trembling.

Mom squatted down to look into his face. "We're just getting ready in case there *is* ever a fire…"

"Which there's not *going* to be!" added Dad, bouncing Leon.

Jayden looked up at the streetlight over the cul-de-sac (which wasn't even on yet because it was only 6:30 in July). "Will it happen in the night?" he asked.

"We don't know," said Mom.

And Dad said at the same time, "It's not *going* to happen!"

Mom stood up straight and glared at Dad, but, just then, Mrs. Kostenko's electric convertible pulled silently into her driveway.

"Is everything all right?" she asked, staring curiously at us lined up on the sidewalk.

"Everything's fine!" said Mom and Dad in unison, turning on their smile-y meet-the-neighbors voices—which was scary enough to send Mrs. Kostenko on into her garage.

Jayden was scared of something else entirely, however.

"I don't want the moon to see me," he said, glancing at the sunny sky. "I don't want to come outside." He grabbed mom's leg again.

"You can't stay inside when there's a fire," I scoffed.

But Mom promised, "Don't worry, honey. We'll have a meeting place that is safe from the man-in-the-moon."

And that's how the five of us ended up on the middle platform (now the lowest platform) of the Dojo, hunkered down inside the tent, escaping from an imaginary fire and hiding from the moon in broad daylight.

It was dim inside the tent and kind of muggy. And there was nothing to do.

"I'm bored," I announced in case anyone was interested.

"I'm hungry," said Jayden.

Leon squealed his protest too.

"Well, if it was a real emergency," said Mom, "we would have brought out the emergency kit, so we would have snacks and flashlights."

Mom looked at Dad, who was letting Leon chew on his phone.

"Honey," she asked, "do we have baby food in the emergency kit?"

Dad looked up at her and answered, "What emergency kit?"

"Don't we *have* an emergency kit?" Mom asked.

Dad shrugged. "Not that I know of. Of course, if it's important to *you*..."

"It's important to *all* of us!" Mom asserted.

"Right. Of course!" said Dad. "That's what I meant."

There was a long silence. Then Dad said, "I guess I'd better take care of that."

It turns out Mom thought Dad would have taken care of that important task because of how he's in charge of all the important maintenance tasks around the house like getting the roof fixed and getting the cars serviced and calling the plumber and complaining about the cost of the plumber and the mechanic and the roofers.

And it turns out Dad had never gotten an emergency kit because…well, it never crossed his mind.

To be fair, Dad was busy—so busy that, the next day, after Mom went to work, he gave me extra screen time so I could find him a kit to order online.

When I did, he complained about the cost of the kit. (So, I guess he was doing his job.)

"It's a racket," Dad said, pointing to the computer screen. "You pay through the nose, and then, if there *is* ever an emergency, you'll open that expensive kit and find half the stuff doesn't work."

I looked suspiciously at the emergency kit on the screen in its red duffel bag with reflective trim.

"We probably have all that stuff around the house anyway," Dad said. Then he snapped his fingers. "I'll pay you half that price to go around and find everything we need to make our own emergency kit. That'll even save me the time and cost of shipping," he said happily. "Not a bad deal," he added, rubbing his hands together, "especially if we should have an emergency right away!"

I was disturbed by Dad's sudden enthusiasm, but I wasn't going to pass up the chance to make a buck.

By the time the dudes came over that afternoon, I already had a pile of emergency supplies—including baby food, of course. Dad was right that I found everything we needed around the house. The trick was to get it all in one container and ready to travel.

Connor agreed. "I always keep some emergency food on me," he said, pulling a hot dog in a baggie out of his pocket to demonstrate.

In the garage, we found an old beige suitcase with wheels. It used to belong to Mr. Dorminter, who lived here before us and left it behind. So I figured Mom wouldn't mind if we used it. There were even a few of his old magazines in there.

"You can always use more reading material in an emergency," said Nate. So we left the old stuff in the suitcase and piled the new stuff on top. There was plenty of room, and the wheels and handles would make it easy to move in an emergency.

Nate wrote: EMERGENCY KIT on the side in sharpie and we were done.

When Dad paid us, Ryan figured this could be a business opportunity.

"I bet there's a lot of people who haven't got their emergency kit together," he said. "Who wouldn't love having us dig through all their closets for flashlights and stuff?"

I wasn't sure about the answer to that question, but Ryan predicted: "All we have to do is get the word out."

Deven had an idea about advertising:

"Mom says there's a guy down at the courthouse who stands on the corner with a sign that says 'Disaster is Nigh!' I know it *sounds* like he mis-spelled 'night'," Deven explained, "but Mom says it's a word that means 'near'."

"It sounds Biblical," I said.

"Some of the best disaster movies come from the Bible!" Ryan pointed out.

"We want to express the urgency, but we don't want to put customers off with unfamiliar words," said Nate.

So that's how the Dudes ended up at Teresa's house, carrying a sign that said "DISASTER IS HERE!"

By the look on her face when she saw us, she believed what she read. But Teresa didn't want an emergency kit. She said they already had one—the kind you buy online.

Then Teacup came tearing out of the house to start gnawing on Ryan's ankle, which gave him a great idea—Ryan, not the dog.

"Do you have a week's worth of supplies for your precious pet?" Ryan asked.

That wiped the smug off Teresa's face.

"Oh!" she said, scooping the Chihuahua into her arms as if to protect him from her own thoughtless neglect. "What if the invisible fence doesn't work? I'll need a cage and a leash and food and water and pooper-scooper bags…" (gag)

She let Teacup lick her nose for a minute. (double gag).

When she faced us again, it was with that determined Teresa look that gives the Dudes nightmares.

"I bet a lot of people haven't thought what their pet will need in an emergency," she said. "We should inform them as a public service."

"Public service?" echoed Ryan.

"You mean we won't get paid?" asked Connor.

"You don't do good to get rich," said Teresa.

"Maybe *you* don't," said Ryan.

"You'd never make money selling pet kits anyway," said Teresa knowledgably. "Every pet eats something different. And people won't pay for food their pet won't eat."

"Maybe she's right," I said. "There are a lot of different kinds of dog and cat food. They have whole stores for it."

"It's expensive too," said Connor.

I nodded. "Almost as expensive as organic baby food."

"We didn't earn enough from Mr. Reynolds to buy pet supplies," Nate pointed out.

"Okay, Teresa," said Ryan, reluctantly, "you got your public service."

11 Dudes Serve the Public

That was Teresa for you: whatever she wanted you to do, she always had an argument for it—a good one. So it wasn't long before Nate was filming a public service announcement with Teresa as the spokesperson, and Teacup as the spokesdog.

Deven had wanted to do it (either part), but he makes an emergency look like too much fun. There's nothing fun about Teresa. Anyway, we figured she and Teacup were bound to scare people into *some* kind of action.

We filmed it a couple blocks away at the construction site for the new Valley View Estates. They had just cleared the lot, and Nate figured the piles of dirt and torn up trees kind of looked like a disaster area.

Our actors did a good job. Teacup's bulging eyeballs gave him sort of a traumatized look. And Teresa was utterly sincere at the end as she looked toward the camera and said,

"Don't you want the *best* for your little one during an emergency?"

It was Teresa's idea to post the message on the Sherwood Spotlight site. They have a section where citizens can post events and comments. It was the biggest section. People could read announcements about the Arts Festival or the Middle School Graduation. Or they could post practical questions and answers like "Anybody know a good furnace guy?" or "How can I keep squirrels from nesting in my attic?"

There were also people like Grandpa who asked things like: "How did the city council slide *that* one by us?" and "What's the mayor up to *now*?"

The next day our public service announcement ran right next to one by the mayor. The mayor's post showed her with a big, toothy smile. The post was just four words in large font: "Something Big is Coming!" (My guess was: a hat.)

The Dudes' post showed our video's featured thumbnail: the picture of that guy on the earthquake pamphlet falling in the crack. Nate had added a clipart dog silhouette that was falling with him. It wasn't exactly accurate. I mean, the guy didn't have his emergency kit with him. He also didn't look like he was going to survive long enough to need it. But the picture was eye-catching and more dramatic than hand sanitizer or Connor's hot dog.

After the picture, we had a reminder about preparing for your pets in an emergency and a link to the video.

The announcement generated quite a few questions and comments:

How do I know how much dog food I need?

In an emergency, do we still have to scoop the poop?

I'm a reporter with the Sherwood Spotlight. I'd like to ask a few questions. Will you contact me?

Remember to include all your pet medications. My baby takes prescription eye drops and pills. He's gluten-free too.

11 Dudes Serve the Public

Mine only takes his pill when it's wrapped in bacon. Don't know what I'll do with a bunch of raw bacon in an emergency.

I heard bacon was poisonous for dogs.

I think that's chocolate.

Oh, Sherman isn't a dog. He's a python.

After reading the comments and watching our video again, Nate said, "It's not very exciting, but I think we can feel good that we raised awareness of the needs of pets in an emergency."

"I just wish we hadn't raised my awareness of a hungry python in the neighborhood," I said.

"Hey! A reporter wants to interview us," Ryan pointed out. "Let's call him up."

"Teresa's our spokesperson," Nate pointed out.

"But she's not here," Ryan countered.

That was true. We were at Deven's house today looking at the Spotlight on the laptop in his dad's office.

Deven grabbed the phone and hugged it to his chest.

"You gotta be careful when talking to the press," he warned us. "They'll twist your words and incriminail you."

"I'll be careful," Ryan promised.

Deven gave him the phone, advising, "Just answer his questions and don't evaporate."

Nate frowned. "I think you mean 'elaborate'," he suggested.

"I know what I'm talking about," Deven insisted. "My mom's a lawyer, and she interrogates me about *something* practically every week. Just answer 'yes' or 'no' and then shut your mouth."

Ryan sat down at Mr. Singh's desk and dialed the Spotlight offices. Deven stood close by. The rest of us lounged on Mr. Singh's napping couch or perused his collection of golf videos on DVD which stood in neat rows on a bookcase by the door.

When the reporter answered, Ryan put him on speaker so we all could listen.

"Are you the person or persons involved with the post on the Citizen Spotlight site this morning?" asked the reporter.

"Yes," said Ryan and shut his mouth.

Deven nodded approvingly.

"Can you give me an idea what it's all about?" asked the reporter.

"Yes," said Ryan.

"Good," said the man. "Tell me everything."

Ryan raised his eyebrows. How was he supposed to give a one word answer to that?

"Don't..." started Deven and slapped his hands over his mouth.

"What was that?" asked the reporter.

"Nothing!" shouted Nate.

"You're not talking?" asked the reporter. "Then why did you make the post?"

Ryan shrugged, so I jumped in.

"It's a public service," I said.

"Then you feel there is something the people need to know!" said the reporter excitedly.

Ryan smiled. "Yes!" he answered confidently.

"Can you make a comment on the record about the warehouse on River Street?" the reporter asked.

Ryan looked around at our blank faces. "Uh, no?" he answered.

"What would you say to someone who complains about the large amount of money involved?" asked the reporter.

Ryan leaned forward. "Look, dog food is pretty expensive," he asserted.

"But it's still cheaper than organic baby food!" Connor put in.

"Don't you want the best for your little one during an emergency?" quoted Deven in a high, girly voice.

There was a pause while, I guess, the reporter was trying to figure out who had said what.

"This is great, but I may need more," he said at last. "Can I contact you again at this number?"

"Huh? No!" yelled Ryan. He pushed the off button and shoved the phone across the table to Deven. "Do you think he traced the call?"

"Probably just used caller ID," said Nate. "We should have thought to use a public phone."

"Or the one at Teresa's house," suggested Connor.

"Boy, did you notice how he asked those trick questions to get us to say more than one word?" said Ryan.

Deven nodded. "He was a real pro."

"I think it's okay, guys," I said. "I mean we didn't say anything but the truth. It's probably good publicity for Nate's film."

"Yeah," said Ryan, relaxing into Mr. Singh's office chair. "We totally nailed it."

12 Dudes Safe Room

"Filming the public service announcement has piqued my interest in making a disaster movie of some kind," said Nate as we recovered from talking to the press. "Creating a catastrophe on film would be exhilarating."

"What about filming a flood?" suggested Connor.

"Kowabunga Dude!" agreed Deven.

But Nate shook his head. "My dad's camera isn't waterproof," he explained. "Besides, a tsunami isn't very likely in Sherwood Heights. We're too far from the ocean. We are much more likely to suffer a power outage due to inclement weather."

Deven turned off the lights and pulled down the shades in his Dad's office. Even then, the room wasn't really dark because of the light coming around the window edges and streaming in under the door from the skylight in the hall.

Nate got the camera out of his backpack and took a short video. "I think I need to find a disaster that has more visual appeal," he said, staring at the black screen.

"The Dudes will help," I promised.

"Yeah," added Ryan, "Disasters are our specialty."

Then Deven led us out to the kitchen where we could eat while thinking.

From the living room, Deven's grandmother called, "Eat the healthy snacks on the table," without ever looking up from the video screen where it still leaned against a potted plant on the floor.

"Thanks, Nani," said Deven, kissing her cheek and dodging as she shooed him away with one hand and stitched a cushion cover with the other.

"I must watch this silly movie or else what will I talk to my sister about on the SKYPE?" she complained.

In the kitchen, we sat around the table, which was conveniently loaded with edamame dip and pita chips and grapes. Deven's grandmother is pretty serious about healthy eating, but she's also a good cook, so we didn't mind choking down the fiber and vitamins. It wasn't like the gluten-free crackers and coconut water at Nate's house. Of course, it wasn't like the cheese doodles and frozen pizza at Ryan and Connor's house either. I guess that's why they say it takes a village to raise a Dude.

Just then we heard the rumble of the garage door and Mr. Singh came into the kitchen.

"I have had a very tiring day," he said to no one in particular as he slipped off his loafers at the door. Then he looked up and saw the Dudes. "Deven, why are you here?" he said. "What are you and your friends doing?" he added suspiciously.

"We're preparing for incompetent weather, Dad," said Deven.

Mr. Singh frowned and started toward the living room. But he stopped when he saw the happy people singing and dancing on the video screen. Changing his mind, he whirled and strode the other direction.

"I will be in my office," he said, shutting the door.

When he was gone, the Dudes got back to work.

"There must be a more interesting disaster than a power outage," Ryan said.

Nate pulled the emergency pamphlets out of his backpack. "Actually, I was interested in doing a volcano movie," he said. "My mom still has the working volcano model I built in kindergarten. I could replenish the chemicals and film it erupting on close-up."

"Lava-rific!" said Deven.

I picked up the volcano pamphlet. "What's this 'shelter in place'?" I asked, reading the cover.

"It's a plan to keep you safe from a chemical spill or volcanic ash," Nate explained. "You know, when Mt. St. Helens erupted in 1980, the ash plume reached 15 miles high. If Mt. Rainier were to erupt…"

"Cool!" said Connor and Ryan together.

"Let's prepare for *that*," said Deven.

"This says to create a 'safe room'," I read.

"Yes. A room with only one entrance and a connecting bath would be ideal," said Nate.

"Dad's office has a bathroom," Deven volunteered.

Nate nodded. "It also has a phone and computer to keep up with emergency information."

"—and Zombie Bash updates!" added Connor.

Nani paused her movie to find us some tape and black plastic trash bags which we took outside to seal the windows.

"The water supply will come from the bathroom," said Nate.

"What about food?" asked Connor, patting his pockets.

Nate got a few of the energy bars his mom makes him keep in his backpack and slid them under the door. It wasn't much of a sacrifice. Nate says they taste like they're made of tar sprinkled with rocks.

Then he rolled a towel and laid it in front of the door so no noxious fumes would seep in through the crack.

"Okay, it's the moment of truth," said Deven, opening skype on his phone. "We'll call the victim and see how the safe room is working."

We could hear the blooping through the door. Then the camera started working and we could see…well, not much in the dark room except Mr. Singh's forehead illuminated by the bluish light of the computer screen.

"Dad!" said Deven.

"Deven? Why are you calling?" asked Mr. Singh. He rubbed his eyes. "Am I dreaming?"

12 Dudes Safe Room

He stumbled across the room to the window and opened the shades but our black plastic was blocking the light (as well as any toxic fog.)

"How long did I nap?" Mr. Singh mumbled.

"You're in the safe room, Dad," Deven explained patiently. Then he read from the pamphlet. "Please shelter in place and stay tuned to your local stations for announcements about when the disaster will be over."

"Disaster?!" Mr. Singh squatted and covered his head. Then he peered at the computer from under his arms. "What has happened? Deven, are you all right, son?"

He squinted at the screen and we were treated to a scary close-up of Mr. Singh's nose.

"Why is there sunshine where you are?" he asked.

He stood up and strode toward the door.

I heard Mr. Singh's yelps as he stepped on the energy bars. But by the time he had gotten the door open and tripped over the towel and his eyes had adjusted to the sun coming in the skylight, the emergency was over, and the Dudes were long gone

13 A Dudes Production

The next day, we took over Deven's living room to test out the new TV with Zombie Bash III: Space Station Offensive.

"Offensive is right!" said Ryan, beheading a zombie and watching it use its tongue to launch its head toward him across the airlock.

"That's only possible in zero g," Connor asserted.

We were celebrating Nate's good news: His mother had seen our public service announcement on the neighborhood website. She had decided he could enter it in the Young Journalist category of the film production contest at the Arts Festival, which meant Nate could stop trying to make a meaningful film and start using his creative energies for having fun.

We'd been ignoring Deven's grandmother who was doing something on the patio, but, unfortunately, she wasn't ignoring us. Now she set down her electric drill and stepped through the glass door.

"I find this game so unrealistic," she announced, unplugging the TV.

"Aw! Nani..." said Deven.

(This was the problem with being supervised. Adults are so judgmental.)

"Do not start to plead, Deven," she warned him. Her sari slid down her arm as she lifted the screen from the floor. "You should be spending your free time in more productive pursuits."

The Dudes sat there blinking while Deven's grandmother carried the flat screen out the patio door and hung it on the wall.

"Uh, Nani?" Deven finally said, "How come you put the TV outside?"

Nani smiled and gestured around the patio. "I am creating an outdoor room which will enhance the value and entertaining versatility of the home," she explained. "I saw this on Luxury Outdoor Living," she added.

"You mean LOL?" asked Connor.

"It's one of Nani's programs," Deven explained to the rest of us.

The outdoor room was just what it sounded like. Besides the TV, there was a barbecue and mini fridge for outdoor snacking, a huge sofa and deep chairs (with the new cushions Nani had made from Deven's muscles) for outdoor slouching, and potted plants and long curtains for outdoor privacy. There was even a bowl of decorative moss on the coffee table—in case you forgot what nature looked like. In fact, you could do almost everything you could do inside except without walls and a roof.

Come to think of it, it kinda reminded me of the Dudes' treehouse dojo—except we had dart guns instead of candles and vases. Anyway, the dojo is where we went after Nani told us the TV wouldn't work until tomorrow when the electrician arrived to install the outdoor connections.

On the way, I said to Deven, "Your grandmother is right that the game's not realistic. How would zombies get into orbit anyway?"

"It explains in the cut scene, remember?" said Connor. "The shuttle crew wasn't infected until after they left earth—when that sample container broke."

Ryan nodded. "The pilot tried to warn the station, but the second-in-command ate his brain before he could send the message."

"NASA needs a protocol to detect and blast ships full of zombies out of the sky *before* they dock," Nate mused.

"Zombies would be pretty easy to beat if people could always use their brains," Connor realized.

"Robots would make a much better foe for mankind," said Nate. "They use tools and weapons, they are intelligent, and their brains are inedible."

"And they *explode* when you shoot them instead of oozing," Deven agreed.

"Robots are even more immortal than the undead," said Nate. "In the face of resistance, robots would devise a way to transfer their intelligence and experience to a newly manufactured body."

"You think like a robot, Nate," I told him.

"Thanks," said Nate.

Of course, now that the pressure was off, Nate found his inspiration.

"I should have made a robot invasion movie!" he lamented.

Ryan shrugged. "Let's do it now," he said.

"Who's going to be the robot?" asked Connor suspiciously, "I don't want to have to wear a trashcan or something."

"We already have a robot," said Nate.

"No offense Nate," I said, "but your remote control robot is kind of small to invade the earth. It didn't even scare Teacup."

"I accept your challenge," Nate answered. "With the right filming techniques, I believe I can create an invasion worth fleeing."

The next day Nate was still confident.

"A single robot is stronger than a human," he said, gesturing to his remote control robot.

"Stronger than my pinkie maybe," said Deven, holding out his finger.

"Ow!" he cried when the robot claw closed on it.

"The army could beat that thing in no time," argued Ryan, keeping his fingers away.

"Robots are technical experts," said Nate. "Suppose they hijacked all transmissions and prevented humanity from organizing their forces until it was too late?"

"That's beginning to sound like an invasion," I said approvingly.

"I recorded this sound file last night," Nate said, clicking a file marked: Reporter.

There was a burst of static and some clicks. Then Nate's voice, cutting in and out of the background noise:

"In all my years as a reporter, I never thought I'd be covering the end of humanity. I don't know how much time I have until they discover this frequency and home in to shut me down. They're destroying everything, everyone. If you're still free, get out of the city...hide, find a way to fight back...(there was a burst of static, then the voice came back weaker and higher pitched.) They're here! They've found me! If you can hear this...Nooo!

The recording ended with a weird humming sound, then a crash, and silence.

"That was awesome, Dude," said Ryan. "I would be totally freaked if that was real!"

"I find killer robots inspiring," said Nate modestly. "But I need video to go with the sound," he said.

So the Dudes went out to scout locations. That's movie lingo for finding places that look like they were destroyed by invading robots. It's not as easy as you might think.

We started at the construction site where we had filmed Teresa and Teacup to see if we could find something even scarier than they are.

We were in luck. There was a big digger trundling around making tracks in the soft dirt as well as a lot of noise.

Nate took some video of the digger's huge tank-like tracks. If his robot were really that size, it would be pretty scary.

As the digger turned away, Ryan and Connor ran behind it, weaving from side-to-side serpentine fashion as if they were dodging death rays. Ryan carried the Elephant Gun. As we watched, he braced himself against the pile of pink brick that was once the farmhouse. He pulled the trigger and pumped off a round toward the "robot".

Then Connor shouted "Look out!" and both boys threw themselves behind the pile of bricks.

13 A Dudes Production

Nate was getting a shot of the piles of rubble when the digger shut down suddenly.

"What's going on?" shouted the foreman, striding out of the office trailer. "Why'd you stop work, Joe?"

"Something knocked my hat off," complained the driver.

The foreman looked around at Deven and Nate and me.

"You kids aren't supposed to be here," he said.

Nate kept filming while Joe jumped down from the cab and crawled between the treads to reach for something. He came out with his cap and a bright orange dart.

"I'll take that, mister," shouted Ryan.

Both the men jumped as Ryan and Connor appeared from behind the piles of brick wielding a huge purple gun.

The driver grudgingly handed the dart back to Ryan. "Could have put my eye out," he complained.

"Not unless I wanted to," Ryan responded fiercely, his eyes gleaming from under the brim of his adventure hat.

The foreman stepped between them. "You kids get out of here," he said angrily. "It's dangerous."

Then he turned to the other guy. "Joe? What are you doing up here anyway?" he asked, unfurling a roll of construction plans. As we walked away, I heard him say, "You're supposed to be working the northeast corner not the southeast."

Nate reviewed the video he'd made. "I was afraid of that," he said. "The purple and green of the Elephant Gun is too unrealistic. I can't use the shooting scene."

You have to hand it to Nate. He has high standards.

Connor had noticed something else. He pointed to the scene of the demolished brick farmhouse.

"It's the same pink brick as the new bathrooms at the splash park," he said.

"Grandad says everything old comes back into fashion eventually," I told him. (That's why grandad still wears the shoes he bought in 1997.)

Nate got a gleam in his eye. "I can use this coincidence," he said.

So we went to the splash park to film a scene of the bathrooms.

"I'll add explosion sounds and laser effects to make it look like the robot turned this wall into a pile of rubble with its high tech weapon," Nate explained.

Then he started filming one of the newly installed art exhibits—a sculpture of twisting metal tubes. According to the plaque, it was called "Dignity".

A man with bushy hair who must have been the artist rushed over. "This is my gift to the community of Sherwood," said the man proudly.

"Thank you," said Nate politely. Then he added, "On a background of stars, this will look like a robot mothership in orbit."

The artist frowned, but Nate grinned. His film was coming together.

14 Dudes About Town

Artists were all over town that week. The Arts Festival is Sherwood's biggest event, and it's always an opportunity to see all the art you can stomach. Luckily for the Dudes, it's also an opportunity for local restaurants to set up booths offering snacks with artsy names.

On Saturday, I got Picasso Popcorn and wandered around the festival with Ryan, Connor, and Deven.

We found Nate near the Frida Kahlo Fried Bananas.

"How's the video going?" I asked.

"I cut some scenes together last night," Nate replied. "We can go to my house later to watch it."

Suddenly Nate's mother rushed up.

"Nathaniel, did you get some lunch?" asked Mrs. Howe. She handed him a package of El Greco Granola.

"Mom!" said Nate, slapping his forehead. "I forgot to give you the flash drive of the public service announcement!"

His mom's red lipstick stretched in a fond smile. "Don't worry, dear. I know how busy you are (by which she meant how absent-minded he is), so I copied it off your computer last night. I've already submitted it."

"Whew," said Nate, taking a sip of his Surrealist Smoothie as his Mom rushed off to find the Chairman.

Deven stopped to get a Rembrandt Wrap. Then we explored the festival.

It wasn't any more boring than usual, really. But it *was* hotter. The most common request at the origami booth was for folding fans, and the face-painting was dripping off kids' cheeks.

The theme of the festival this year was Art for Community. Jayden had certainly done his part. His painted benches were very popular among the community as seating for small children and shade for small dogs.

The bushy artist from the splash park was there overseeing an interactive exhibit he called "Symbology". Basically, it was traffic signs with Velcro parts to make their numbers, arrows, and even colors changeable. That would have confused things if all the downtown streets weren't closed anyway.

"I wonder why they closed the streets this year," I said. "They never did that before."

"Mom said there's going to be a surprise," Nate informed us.

"Maybe it's a parade," Connor guessed. His lips were still purple from his Van Gogh Grape snow cone.

We went inside the community center, where the kids' paintings were set up on easels.

There was a photography exhibit too. This was mostly pictures of nature, but Nate and I stopped to look at some close-ups of bricks and mortar with the title "Building Community".

The photographer walked up to us. "It's not the bricks that make the community, see, it's the people gathering to look at them," he said.

"Deep," Nate commented.

Nate had a theory that talking about art is the same as talking to reporters: you're safer if you restrict yourself to one-word answers.

"Yeah, well," said the photographer. "I think most of the community is in here for the air conditioning today," he admitted.

It was cool inside, but you couldn't eat in there, so the Dudes had to leave eventually.

"Look, at that screen!" said Ryan as we came out onto the big lawn in front of City Hall. "Now this is what I call luxury outdoor living!" he said.

"I hope Nani doesn't see it," said Deven.

But no one could miss this screen. Nate's mom had arranged for a giant screen to cover the front of City Hall. On it were playing the Young Filmmaker video entries.

Crowds stood in clumps watching the Young Journalist entries which were on the screen now. Mostly kids reported on recycling efforts or interviewed their grandparents. The public service announcement with Teresa and Teacup definitely stood out from the rest.

I turned away from the giant image of Teacup but found myself looking at the real thing. Only now the Chihuahua was wearing a tiny artist's smock and beret.

"I entered our video," said Teresa, waving Teacup's little paw.

"Then what did Mom enter?" wondered Nate.

"Don't worry," said Teresa graciously, "Teacup and I will share the prize with you if we win."

After the Young Journalist Category, art films came on the screen.

We watched a blurry montage of birds.

"Colorful," Deven said.

In the next film, water flowed in a stream then out of a spout and then became paint splashing over someone's face.

"Wet," said Connor.

I couldn't tell if Teresa was impressed with our art analysis, but Teacup had curled up under one of Jayden's benches and gone to sleep.

The next film portrayed a ring of trees, rustling their leaves in the wind around a fountain.

I recognized the fountain from the Country Club, and nudged Ryan.

"What's so funny?" asked Teresa as the Dudes sniggered.

"We're just thinking about some 'deer' friends of ours," Ryan explained.

Next up was a video of girls whirling in the dark in glow-y white dresses. At least, I assumed it was girls. You could really only see the dresses.

"Spooky," said Nate.

But Ryan couldn't resist adding, "Is this what you and your friends do at night, Teresa? It would explain why you're so dizzy."

The girls went on spinning, and Connor complained, "These movies need more action. If I had a body camera, I could make an awesome movie the next time Dad takes us skiing."

"Yeah, call it 'Avalanche'!" suggested Ryan, dodging as Connor slashed at him with his DaVinci Dog on a Stick.

Luckily, there was a tapping on the microphone just then and everyone directed their attention to where Art the Owl stood at the top of the City Hall steps.

The owl didn't speak but waved his wings toward a man wearing a suit with a ribbon on his lapel.

"That's Uncle Miguel!" said Teresa, clapping. "He's the chairman this year!"

Uncle Miguel cleared his throat and spoke nervously into the microphone.

"I'm glad you all came out today to see how art brings the community together!" said Uncle Miguel.

The audience clapped for themselves.

"Now I'd like to ask one of the heroes of our community to come up here and say a few words."

The Dudes hoped it would be Captain America or something, but it was just the mayor, who shook Mr. Lopez's hand and took the microphone gracefully.

The mayor smiled and waved at the crowd. When the applause died down, she spoke smoothly.

"If you've seen my signs around town and on the Sherwood Community webpage, you know that 'Something Big is Coming'!" she said.

"I thought that meant her hat," muttered Ryan.

"Today is the day you'll find out the truth," the mayor announced confidently.

The reporters in town must have liked that idea because a bunch of people with cameras and recorders converged around her on the steps.

"Are you finally going to tell us how you spent the city's emergency funds?" shouted one woman.

"You'll find out all about…" began the mayor, but another question cut her off.

"Did you or did you not use city funds to rent a warehouse on River Street?" asked another reporter.

"I had a good reason..." the mayor tried again.

"Mayor!" shouted someone else. "Do you have a pet?"

The mayor looked confused.

"Why, yes. I..."

"Would you put that pet's survival above the health of someone else's baby?"

The mayor hesitated, the smile frozen on her face.

Deven shook his head.

"She should have stuck with one-word answers," he said.

"Yeah. She's evaporating," said Connor.

Then a familiar voice shouted, "Mayor, can you confirm rumors that the city now owns a warehouse full of emergency kits with dogfood in them?"

15 Dudes Invasion

The crowd gasped.

So did the mayor. "What on earth...who told you that?" the mayor demanded.

"My source spoke under cover of anonymity," said the reporter.

The crowd muttered.

The Dudes shrugged.

But the mayor laughed. "I'll be happy to show you all what's in the warehouse," she said, checking her watch. "In fact, it should be here any minute."

Sure enough, something big was coming, and it wasn't a parade. We heard a rumble from the direction of River Street. Everyone turned to see the police opening the barricade to let a huge RV turn onto Main Street. It cruised down the closed street and pulled up to the curb in front of City Hall.

"This," announced the mayor, triumphantly, "is Sherwood's new Mobile Emergency Command Center."

She wasn't lying. The words Mobile Emergency Command Center were written in blue on the side of the enormous day-glo yellow vehicle. It had several antennae and a satellite dish on top, and, as we watched, the sides slid out to make the thing twice as wide.

"It has a conference room and is equipped with redundant forms of communication," said the Mayor. "This vehicle will support the needs of multiple first responders during any sort of emergency situation the city of Sherwood might face," she promised.

The crowd murmured.

"Cool," said Ryan.

A more natural smile had returned to the mayor's face. "I'll be happy to answer any questions, but I want everyone to get a good look—especially the press," she said. "The Mobile Emergency Command Center will be open for tours in a few minutes."

The Dudes were anxious to see it, and we were just about to get in line when we heard gasps from behind us.

"Look!" shouted someone, pointing above the mayor, where the art video screen was still playing.

The ghost girls had finally stopped spinning, and I couldn't tell what had taken their place. Whoever took the video was shaking the camera—or maybe the world was shaking because we heard a loud rumble and then a kind of spitting sound like static.

The camera showed shaky, short glimpses of broken trees, fallen bricks,...and *tank tracks*.

Yep, it was Nate's robot invasion movie.

"...I don't know how much time I'll have until they discover this frequency and home in to shut it down," said the voice on the video amid scenes of destruction.

"Who is that?" asked someone behind me.

"Is this for real?" asked someone else.

"He must have broken into the video feed," said someone who sounded knowledgeable.

"They're destroying everything..." said the voice on the video as a wall was reduced to rubble.

"Where is that happening?" asked a voice.

"Was that the splash park?" said someone, pointing to the tumble of pink brick.

15 Dudes Invasion

"My 'Dignity' is there!" cried the man with bushy hair.

The crowd gasped at a quick glimpse of Joe's legs sticking out from under a pair of huge tracks.

"Can we help him?" asked a lady.

Then came a shout. "Somebody call the police!"

The film ended with one brief flash of Nate's robot, filmed from below so it would look like it was towering over the camera. The view was cloudy because it had been shot through a haze of flour (which the Dudes had been puffing toward the camera and which Connor had inhaled, inducing a choking fit which had caused him to bump into Nate who had then dropped the camera).

On the screen, it looked like...well, like a robot invasion.

People looked at the mayor, at each other, then back at the screen, but the loop had restarted, and there were only scenes of recycling and smiling old people.

"This is a job for Superman!" Jayden shouted.

But the mayor had a different idea.

"My fellow citizens, I'm sure there is nothing to be alarmed about," she said uncertainly. "Just the same, this is an excellent opportunity to make use of our new mobile command center."

The rest of what she said was drowned by a siren as the police jumped in their squad car. The mayor handed off the microphone to Art the Owl and trotted down the steps on her high heels. She hopped into the Command Center vehicle and rode off to respond to the attack on our town's family restrooms.

Since Art the Owl doesn't speak, he handed the microphone to Teresa's uncle.

"Well, uh…Everyone should please remain calm…," said Uncle Miguel over the microphone.

But people weren't listening or remaining. Kids wanted to go fight robots—or at least go to the splash park. Parents wanted to beat the traffic out of the parking lot. And the rest of the crowd, I figured, just wanted to see something more interesting than dresses spinning in the dark.

"Mom must have got the wrong video file," Nate guessed.

The Dudes had figured that out.

Connor and Deven headed over to Mona Lisa's Munchies, which now had no line. Ryan and Nate and I wandered back to the air conditioned photography exhibit.

"Why didn't you go to the splash park with the others?" asked the photographer.

"There's nothing to see there," Nate answered.

"I know," said the photographer. "I recognized the rubble in the film." He gestured toward his photographed bricks, and I realized where I'd seen them before. Only he must have taken his pictures before the farmhouse was torn down.

"Showing the movie was a mistake," Nate started to explain.

But the photographer stopped him. "Never apologize for your work," he advised. "Look how your art brought the community together. You should win the top prize!"

Nate didn't win any prizes because his mom had entered his fictional robot film in the Journalism category. But his art did bring the community together. The <u>Sherwood Spotlight</u> page was active for days with posts arguing whether his movie was art or just a prank and whether the Mobile Emergency Command Center was a useful piece of equipment or a waste of (Grandad's) money. His mom said the discussion he generated would help give new life to the Arts Festival for years to come!

16 Dudes Power Down

"They have the full specs for the Mobile Emergency Command Center on the city website," said Nate, clicking fast through the site on his laptop.

It was a Sunday afternoon, and Nate and I were in the dojo, sprawled on the old cushions Deven's grandmother had given us when she finished redecorating the yard. Ryan was using a cushion too—as a target for practicing with the Elephant Gun.

We still had Mr. Maguire's inner tubes, so Deven was lounging on Tina's with his feet in the baby pool. Connor had turned his on edge and was trying to roll across the yard inside it.

"What's that periscope thingy?" I asked, looking over Nate's shoulder at the picture on the screen.

"It's a telescopic mast with video capability," said Nate, reading off the screen. Then he turned to me. "Basically, it's a periscope," he answered.

"Awesome, can the MECC go underwater?" asked Connor, his voice bouncing as the tube bounced over the grass.

"I don't think so," said Nate, frowning. "Though, an amphibious vehicle *would* be useful in a flood."

He pointed to the picture of a policewoman. "It says here she's certified to *drive* the MECC, not to pilot a water craft."

"I hope she can swim," said Deven, splashing with his toes.

"It says here 'The Mobile Emergency Command Vehicle offers redundant communications across all frequencies for deploying manpower and equipment regardless of the emergency,'" Nate read.

"As long as they stick to high ground," Connor added. Now he was hugging the outside of the tube as he rolled—basically, practicing being roadkill.

16 Dudes Power Down

"'Its state-of-the-art conference room has satellite television and multiple screens to assist after-action analysis and debriefing,'" Nate went on.

"I'd like to see the after-action analysis on the robot invasion last week," I said, and the Dudes laughed. (And Connor smashed a molehill with his head.)

"Hey, the screen froze!" said Nate, clicking to no effect.

Before anyone could answer, Dad came storming out of the shed—I mean his office. (On weekends, *he* likes to relax by working.)

"Boys, do you have anything to do with the internet cutting out?" he asked. He glanced suspiciously at Connor, lying under the inner tube, then crossed his arms and looked up in the tree.

"No, Mr. Reynolds, honest!" Ryan answered. "We're just as web-less as you are."

"It's probably a problem with your network," said Nate, setting down the laptop. "I could take a look at your router."

Dad had already whipped out his phone to check for an update.

"Never mind," he said. "It looks like Prospective Internet is down." Dad shoved his phone back in his pocket. "That will affect everybody in the neighborhood—unless they happen to get their internet through a satellite TV service."

"Gee, that's too bad," said Ryan, dropping the Elephant Gun. "Come on, Dudes," he added, jumping down from the dojo and waiting while Nate slid his laptop into his backpack. "We gotta go. See you later, Mr. Reynolds."

Ten minutes later, the Dudes were relaxing in outdoor luxury at Deven's house.

"Dad got satellite TV last year," Deven explained. "He says it's so Nani can watch movies from India, but he mainly wanted the golf package."

Nate was checking social media. "There are a lot of posts about the lack of internet service in Sherwood Heights," he said. "I guess people are using their phones to complain about their computers. Someone says there is a Prospective Internet truck across from Hilltop Park."

"That's near the construction site," I pointed out.

"I bet old Joe got confused again and cut an internet cable with his backhoe," said Ryan. He sounded kind of

16 Dudes Power Down

friendly with the guy after having threatened to put his eye out. But then, violence is sort of Ryan's social media.

Just then, Mr. Singh stepped outside the sliding glass door.

"This is the best idea your grandmother ever had," he said to Deven as he crossed to the little square of grass beside the patio with a golf club in his hand. He raised and lowered the putter over a golf ball while watching a tutorial on the flat screen TV.

"Watching the PGA Championship this afternoon with the smell of the grass will be almost like being there," raved Mr. Singh. "Better! Because I can practice during commercials." He gestured toward the outdoor kitchen. "And I have lemonade and iced tea at the ready."

"Sounds good," said Connor, getting up to check the mini-fridge.

"It's not for you," cautioned Mr. Singh. "I am chilling them to make Arnold Palmers."

"Make Arnold Palmers do what?" Ryan asked.

"It's a golf drink," Deven explained.

"You should name them after somebody famous, Mr. Singh," Ryan suggested, "maybe a Dude!"

Mr. Singh paid Ryan no attention as he knocked the ball into a little electronic putting cup. Then he put down the golf club and pulled out his phone to check the related app.

"Yes! I am up a percentage point since last month!" he crowed.

While he was absorbed with his phone, Deven sneaked over and started dropping the ball into the cup over and over.

"What? How can this be?" said Mr. Singh, frowning at the app.

When he looked up, Deven panicked and tossed the ball over his shoulder, where it caromed off the flat screen and landed in a vase of flowers, splashing water onto the table where Ryan was resting his feet.

"Water hazard!" shouted Ryan, slinging water off his shoes.

Meanwhile, Mr. Singh nearly turned inside out as he watched the doom of his outdoor TV turn into the triumph of the screen protector Nani had bought.

"Ha, ha!" said Mr. Singh, clapping his hands. "Your grandmother is a genius."

"That's Nani," said Deven proudly.

16 Dudes Power Down

Then, suddenly, the TV screen went dead.

"What?" said Mr. Singh.

We all stared at the black screen—not even a *No Signal* message.

"Your wi-fi is down too," said Nate, tapping the computer.

Mr. Singh squatted down and put his hand on the fridge like he was checking a patient. "The refrigerator is not humming," he said.

It was Ryan who finally diagnosed the problem. "The power's out."

"Huh?" said Deven.

"How come it's not dark?" said Connor.

"Because we're outside in the daytime," I reminded him.

"Yes, day," said Mr. Singh, looking around. "There is no storm, no wind." He glared into the sky above him and clenched his fists, wailing, "It's a perfect day for golf!"

17 Dudes Offline

"First the internet and now the power," said Ryan, fanning himself with his hat.

Nate nodded. "If I were a robot, this is exactly how I would start my invasion."

Luckily, Nate was on our side. He packed up his backpack again and suggested we go to the construction site to check on old Joe and the foreman.

"Wait for me," said Mr. Singh, dropping his putter. "I must see for myself what is being done to remedy the problem."

We went out the back way from the Singhs' yard and down the neighborhood trail to Hilltop Park, which happens to be across the street from the construction site. The park is unofficially known as Sherwood Forest—although the only trees are spindly maples with wires still holding them up. The real trees were across the street, clinging to the sides of an overgrown ravine that cut steeply down the hill beside the Valley View Estates construction project.

When we arrived, it wasn't too hard to see what had happened. Joe's digger had cut a cable, like we figured. The Prospective Internet truck had showed up in a hurry. Only they appeared to have backed into an electrical tower, bending it and snapping lines leading to what Nate called a "power transfer station" which sat behind a tall fence on the other side of the park.

"This station provides power to all the houses on the hill," Nate explained. "My guess is that a new tower will have to be installed and the lines fixed before electricity can be restored."

"How long?" demanded Mr. Singh. "How long will that take?"

"It could take hours or even days," Nate replied.

"The kid's probably right," said a guy with Prospective Internet embroidered on his shirt pocket.

"Probably?" muttered Nate.

Mr. Singh groaned. "The satellite will not work without electricity and it is almost time for the tee-off."

"Try watching it on your phone, Dad," Deven suggested.

Mr. Singh took out his phone and began wandering around the park looking for the best signal.

"Maybe we should post a message on the <u>Sherwood Spotlight</u>, telling what we know," suggested Nate, "as a public service."

Nate used Deven's phone to take a picture of the electric tower leaning crazily against the "View Homes Coming Soon!" sign with the stalled backhoe in the background. The whole construction catastrophe was already roped off.

"Lucky the construction crew had so much caution tape," Connor said.

"They probably keep extra for Joe the way Mom keeps bandages for you," said Ryan.

While the Maguires began their usual slugfest on the sidewalk, Nate and I looked down the steep hillside separating Sherwood Heights from downtown Sherwood. Below, I could see the broad, flat roof of the Tasty Grocery Mart. In its huge parking lot, sat a Sherwood police car, probably there to buy a tasty lunch. I was getting a little hungry myself.

"Not much of a view," I pointed out.

"I think the view is over there," said Nate, pointing across the valley and over the next ridge. Through a cleft between a hill and an office park, I could see a glimpse of the snow-capped Cascade Mountain Range. Of course, that would only be visible on a rare clear and sunny day like this one. But I've noticed grown-ups tend to see what they want to see—especially if they're paying extra for it.

Meanwhile, Mr. Singh was getting frustrated. "I cannot get an estimate of the time to restore power because the power company refers me to their website, which will not load on my phone for some reason."

"Probably because they don't want you to yell at them about it," I guessed.

"*My* phone won't work at all," said the Prospective Internet guy forlornly. Then he shrugged. "Of course, *our* service is down up here—the cell tower gets its power from..." he gestured toward the broken lines. "I would take the truck down the hill to call in," he said, "but..." he gestured again toward the truck draped with caution tape. "You don't fool with electricity, you know," he said.

"I must save my battery for the Open. But you can use my landline," said Mr. Singh. "Come. They will listen to you," he said hopefully, leading the man toward his house.

"Land line?" said Ryan, releasing his brother in his disappointment. "There's gotta be a better way to send a message outside the zone of the disaster," he said.

"Hmm," said Nate, staring down the hill. "I have an idea, but we'll need the Elephant Gun."

Ryan's face lit up. "I'm on it!" he said, running back toward my house.

"I'll also need something to write a message on," said Nate.

"No problem," said Connor, putting a stick of gum in his mouth and handing over the wrapper.

"That won't hold much message," I warned.

"The message has to be small anyway if it's going to clear the barrel," said Nate, digging in his backpack for a pen. Then he got out the first aid kit his mom insisted he keep with him at all times. Inside, he found a small packet labeled "space blanket".

"What is that?" I asked as he unfolded a lightweight, silver rectangle about the size of a sleeping bag.

"I was going to use this to make a solar pizza oven," said Nate, "but this is an emergency."

Meanwhile, Deven's dad returned with the internet guy.

Mr. Singh was trying to use his binoculars to stare at his phone's screen. But he lowered them in disgust, saying, "The ball is invisible!"

"Uh, can we borrow those, Dad?" asked Deven.

Mr. Singh handed over his binoculars just as we heard Ryan's tennis shoes pounding down the sidewalk and saw him coming back carrying the Elephant gun. He was running in a serpentine pattern, in case any robots or, possibly, local residents, were trying to take him out.

Nate explained the plan, attached the message to a dart, and loaded the Elephant Gun.

When Ryan took the first shot, the recoil knocked him backwards, and the elephant dart flew wild into the blackberry thicket.

Nate wrote another message and attached it to our second dart.

"Connor, come here," Ryan ordered in his on-mission voice. This time he braced himself against his brother before firing.

Unfortunately, a breeze tossed the second shot back toward the hill and it landed somewhere deep in the ravine.

"Last chance," I said, attaching Nate's message to the third dart.

Ryan pulled his hat down lower and took aim.

Nate held up a piece of caution tape and watched for it to go slack before giving the signal to shoot.

This time, the dart sailed down the hill to bounce onto the roof of the police car.

"Direct hit!" cheered Connor around the three-piece wad in his mouth.

Down below, the driver got out of the police car.

Using Mr. Singh's binoculars, I could see it was an older cop, one whose stocky build I recognized. Officer Morgan had a stern look on his face as he surveyed the roof of his car for damage.

"He's got the dart," I said. "Now he's looking around."

"Quick!" said Ryan.

Deven and Nate raised the space blanket and angled it to reflect light down the hill.

I saw Morgan squint in our direction as his partner, a young, skinny guy named Officer Racarro walked up with a tray of sandwiches. He set the tray on the roof of the car and looked at the dart his partner handed him.

"They're reading the message!" I said.

"This better work," said Ryan.

As I watched, the cops went into action. The older cop pulled out his radio and barked into it. Meanwhile, Racarro ran around to hop in the passenger seat and start up the siren. The driver got in and the police car pulled out with a squeal of tires. The sandwich tray flew off the roof, spilling its contents in the parking lot behind them.

"Wow, that was awesome," said Ryan.

"What did the note say?" I asked Nate.

Nate smiled. "It said: 'Help. Bring MECC.'"

# 18 Dudevision

In a few minutes we could hear the siren getting closer as the police climbed the hill. And, sure enough, when the flashing lights came into view, we could see behind them the giant neon yellow RV.

The police screeched to a halt in front of the park. The sides popped out of the emergency vehicle. Morgan and Racarro popped out of the squad car too. Then a policewoman—the certified driver from the website—climbed down from the cab of the MECC.

The cops ran toward the construction site, taking in the tilting power pole and the caution tape and Deven's dad wandering around mumbling about the noisy sirens.

"Was that a stroke?" demanded Mr. Singh, staring at his phone. "I cannot see or hear anything."

"Sir? Are you all right?" asked the older policeman. "You should stay away from downed power lines."

Mr. Singh looked up from his phone in confusion.

"He was saying something about a stroke," said Officer Morgan as the two younger cops ran up.

"Maybe he was struck by lightning!" suggested Racarro.

"More likely heat stroke," said Morgan. "It looks like the power's out up here."

"I'm Officer Aziz," said the policewoman gently, taking Mr. Singh by the elbow. "Come along with me, sir, and you can lie down in the air conditioning."

As Deven's dad followed her to the Command Vehicle without looking up from his phone, the older policeman went to talk to the construction foreman and the Prospective Internet guy.

Meanwhile, neighbors were coming from all directions to see what the first responders were responding to. They surrounded Officer Racarro, who clearly didn't know how to respond.

"What's going on, officer?" asked a man.

"I heard sirens," said Mrs. Howe. "Is there an emergency?"

"When's the power going to come back on?" demanded Mrs. Kostenko.

Everyone looked expectantly at the giant emergency vehicle. Officer Racarro turned around and looked at it too.

That's when Officer Morgan stepped in. "I'm told the power company has been informed, and their truck is on the way," he told the crowd. "But it will probably be several hours before the power comes back on. I suggest everybody just relax in the shade while you wait," he said, gesturing to the spindly new trees.

But nobody relaxed anyway.

"Hours!" said Mrs. Kostenko. "The refrigerator!"

"Right," said Mrs. Howe. "Spread the word," she commanded, tapping on her phone as she spoke. "If the power is going to be out, people should eat whatever won't keep."

Some people ran off, and others started arriving who must have already read Nate's community post. They came striding into the park carrying covered containers and coolers.

Mrs. Maguire showed up with plenty of meat for burgers. Grandad had Leon in the baby-pack and a bag of charcoal in the stroller. Mom was pulling Jayden and three jugs of milk in the wagon. The Gutierrezes had watermelon

18 Dudevision

and sodas and Teacup. Mrs. Kostenko returned with leftover potato salad and cold cuts. Nani had cucumbers and yogurt for raita. Deven's mom carried a pitcher of lemonade in one hand and iced tea in the other. And Nate's mom had—you guessed it—hand sanitizer!

Best of all, everybody had ice cream, which we *had* to eat first because it was melting fast.

Turns out, an emergency is a pretty good excuse to party. Of course, the community was happy to share with the police as well as the construction crew and the Prospective Internet guy. Everyone cheered when the power company truck finally arrived, and Grandad put another batch of burgers on the grill for the crew.

Officer Morgan cornered the Dudes at the playground where Nate had climbed to the top of the slide in order to study the antenna array of the MECC.

"You know, son," said the policeman sternly, "this wasn't really the kind of emergency that the MECC is designed for."

"I disagree," said Nate, before I could stop him.

Luckily, Mrs. Gutierrez walked up just then and shook the officer's hand.

"Wonderful public relations stunt, showing up for a neighborhood power outage," she congratulated him. "Shows the police are looking out for us. And we're all curious about this marvelous contraption," she added gesturing to the Command Vehicle.

The policeman looked from the middle school principal to the Dudes.

"We never got our tours at the Arts Festival, you know," Ryan pointed out.

"Yeah," Deven spoke up. "Show us some of those recumbent communications."

"At first I didn't think we needed this thing," said the policeman. Then he gave the Dudes a flinty look, "But, now that I think about it," he said, "maybe it's a good idea for Sherwood to prepare for the unexpected."

So the vehicle's official driver, Officer Aziz, was assigned to introduce the public to the special features of the MECC. The Dudes got the first tour, starting with the Operations Command Center where Connor used a joystick to raise and lower the periscope and scan the picnic area with the mobile camera.

"Cheese doodles at 12 o'clock!" he shouted.

"Let's run some disaster scenarios," suggested Ryan.

"I'm doing that right now," said the driver nervously, removing Dude hands from the master control board.

She pointed to a computer monitor. "This controls the multiple screens in the conference room," said the officer.

"Do they get satellite TV?" asked Nate.

"Yes," said the policewoman, flipping it on as she explained that it could be helpful to keep abreast of news coverage when responding to an emergency.

When we left the Operations Room, we found Mr. Singh cheering a great drive. He had the golf championship on all seven screens. Officer Aziz started to say something, but Deven rushed over.

"Uh, better keep this on, Dad," said Deven, handing his dad the ice pack he had dropped. "You don't want to *relapse*."

"Yes," said Mr. Singh, glancing at the officer, "of course. I must not rush it," he said, weakly, slumping back onto a bench while clutching the remote control.

So Mr. Singh got his golf, and the police got their public relations. Even Grandad admitted that an RV was a good use of tax-payer money. And I think the whole neighborhood learned that, in an emergency, you can't rely on taking care of yourself. You need Dudes.

19 The Dudes and the Bear

We got our power back, but the hot weather continued—which was not what we were used to in the Pacific Northwest. Grown-ups spent a lot of time talking about the dry summer and the forest fires in the mountains.

The outdoor living room at Deven's was stifling, and none of our houses had air conditioning. Even the Dudes were beginning to look forward to the rains coming, though that would mean the end of summer was coming too.

The week after the power outage the Dudes spent most of our time in Ryan and Connor's garage. Their dad was there, so we were totally supervised.

"Three points and in the pocket!" predicted Mr. Maguire, holding a playground ball over his head and taking aim at the rack of baseball bats on the far wall.

He released the ball, and we all watched as the shot arced across the room. But the bar on the garage door opener got in the way, and the ball ricocheted suddenly back, in our faces!

The Dudes ducked as the rubber ball rocketed toward the tool bench behind us, rebounded off the power saw at an angle, and tagged the corner of a set of gorilla shelves, giving them a shimmy which caused a bowling ball to hop out of its cup and roll slowly off the shelf.

Luckily, Mrs. Maguire liked to keep a large supply of paper towels on hand for mishaps (though this may not have been the kind of mishap she had imagined). The supersize pack of paper towels managed to catch and hold the bowling ball, ending Mr. Maguire's turn.

"The garage door thingy, the power saw, and the shelf," said Connor, counting the bounces on his fingers. "You got the three points, Dad, but you missed all the pockets," he pointed out, rescuing the playground ball from behind the bike stand.

The pockets were six empty crates from the warehouse store that we'd scattered around the room.

"I should get points for using an extra ball," protested Mr. Maguire.

19 The Dudes and the Bear

"Yeah, but you didn't get *that* in a pocket either," said Ryan. "No pocket, no points, Dad."

Ryan was a stickler for the rules of Garage Ball. Also, he was winning.

"I guess that bowling ball should have been stored closer to the ground," said Mr. Maguire, averting his gaze from the crushed paper towel rolls.

"It is now," Deven pointed out.

Mr. Maguire sank into one of the folding lounge chairs we'd moved from the patio. With furniture, the garage was almost as luxurious as an outdoor room. Plus, it was cooler than inside the house.

"No windows," Mr. Maguire had explained. "Sort of like a cave. A man cave."

"A Dude cave," Ryan had corrected.

Mr. Maguire took a soda out of the cooler.

"Why did you bring a suitcase, Tyler?" he joked, eyeing Mr. Dorminter's old bag. "Did your folks kick you out?"

"Almost," I said.

I explained how Dad hadn't been too pleased last night when we got home from the cookout at the park to find the house still without power. He was even less pleased when we opened the emergency kit the Dudes had prepared.

"We put in everything he asked for," said Ryan, "food, drinks, flashlights...even babyfood!"

"Right," I said, unzipping the musty old suitcase to reveal two of Jayden's glow-in-the-dark lightsabers, a bag of Fritos, a six-pack of Choco-Sippies, and the candy corn left over from Halloween. (It's a grain.)

"Mom kept the baby food to put in the *new* kit Dad is ordering online," I explained.

"This is what *I* call emergency supplies," said Deven, pouncing on the Fritos like a hungry bear.

Meanwhile, Connor and Ryan began a lightsaber battle.

"At least you had reading material," said Nate, pulling out one of Mr. Dorminter's old magazines. It was called Paranormal LIFE.

"What's a Sasquatch?" asked Deven, spraying Frito crumbs as he pointed to the cover story.

"That's Bigfoot," said Mr. Maguire.

19 The Dudes and the Bear

"Sasquatch is a cryptid," Nate explained. "In other words, it is a legendary creature for which there has never been any conclusive proof."

"But there's a picture right here," said Connor, lowering his guard to pick up a newspaper clipping.

Ryan sliced him in imaginary halves, then we all looked at the photo.

"That is a blurry picture of a shadow," said Nate.

"A smelly shadow," said Connor. "It says here the creature smelled so bad the guy didn't want to get too close."

"This isn't proof," said Nate, pointing to the picture. "It could be a trick of the light or a bear standing on its hind legs."

"That's true," said Ryan. "Dad, tell Nate about that time the lady at the country club danced with a bear."

Mr. Maguire stretched and chuckled like he always does when he's about to tell one of his "true" stories of Sherwood.

"Well, that was a long time ago, boys," said Mr. Maguire, "when wilderness still stretched all the way to the golf course. In fact, it was logging in the mountains that pushed the bear down into people's neighborhoods.

"I don't think the bear *planned* to attend a wedding reception," Mr. Maguire went on, "and the bride's mother *was* sort of near-sighted..." he trailed off as he noticed a fierce look behind Nate's glasses.

"Anyway," he finished suddenly, "bears *are* seen in the neighborhood sometimes. There's proof. All you have to do is check the internet!"

Then he stood up and looked at his watch. "I have to get home, Dudes," said Mr. Maguire, putting on his helmet. He opened the garage door, hopped on his motorcycle, and drove away, passing Mrs. Maguire's minivan with a salute.

The Dudes put innocent looks on our faces while Mrs. Maguire walked by wearing her nurse's scrubs and carrying two bags of groceries.

When she had disappeared into the kitchen to make supper, Ryan said, "Speaking of the wilderness, at some point we have to go back and get the two missing elephant darts."

"I don't know," I said. "Retrieving our darts always seems to lead to trouble."

"Yeah, Officer Racarro didn't even want to give me the *third* one," said Connor. "He said it was evidence. Luckily,

19 The Dudes and the Bear

Officer Morgan said he didn't want to write up a report on that evidence."

"Foam darts are not biodegradable," Nate pointed out. "It would be irresponsible to leave them in the wilderness."

"Blackberries aren't wilderness," said Deven. "Nani says they're invasive weeds."

"They're tasty too," Connor noted.

"It's settled," Ryan declared, taking off his hat to wipe his forehead. "But we'll go in the evening when it's cooler."

So, after supper, the Dudes returned to the Valley View Estates construction site, which was quiet now that Joe and the foreman had gone home.

"This place needs a better name," said Deven. "I'd call it Asphalt View Estates—Or Supermarket Vista!"

In the twilight, Connor stood beside the new power pole, plucking the warm, sweet fruit off a tangle of blackberry vines and feeding his face.

"Over here, guys," said our leader. He had found a place where a tree had been bulldozed, pulling the razor-sharp thorns to one side and leaving an opening in the thicket.

Behind the vines were, well, more vines heaped over bushes and tangling around trees. Long canes reached toward the sky ten feet or more, ready to overtop the next bush or tree or Dude and claim more of the steep slope.

"They've got me!" shrieked Deven, raising his hands as far as he was able in a plea for help.

Connor and I picked our way over and pulled the thorns lose from Deven's socks, shorts, shirt and skin. Nate was the only one who had come prepared, wearing long pants, rain boots, and his mother's garden gloves.

"This is impossible, guys," Connor complained, leaning against the rotting stump of a hemlock that was probably logged decades ago. "We're never gonna get far enough down the hill to find those darts."

But, just past the hemlock stump, we found the way clear. It was almost spooky--no blackberry vines, just ferns and rocks. Fir cones littered the ground beneath the tall, straight trees.

"Come on, Dudes," said Ryan, "we've got a mission." He led the way down one boulder and up the next one.

19 The Dudes and the Bear

The rest of us followed...

...and ran into him when he stopped on the other side of the last big rock.

Ryan put his finger to his lips and pointed to his right where, through the growing shadows, we could see a dark opening in the side of the hill.

"It's a cave," whispered Connor unnecessarily.

"A bear cave," added Deven in an unnaturally (for him) quiet voice.

"I see a dart!" hissed Ryan, and, sure enough, a flash of orange glowed in the twilight from the cleft of a rock near the cave opening.

His eyes on the prize, Ryan edged closer to the cave. He was just reaching toward the rocky cleft when a strange noise stopped him cold.

We all heard it. It was a humming sound that seemed to grow and vibrate, echoing off the rocks around the mouth of the cave.

"Is that a growl?" I whispered.

"Fall back!" hissed Ryan, grabbing the dart and whirling toward us.

The Dudes scrambled out of his way and then reassembled ourselves to race after our leader.

"Leave no man behind!" cried Deven as Ryan bravely led our retreat up the hill.

When we reached the big tree, Ryan swerved into a hole in the thicket and we bolted after him. It was not the way we had come, but, luckily, the new path was reasonably clear of thorns and led up toward the construction site. Lucky too that no one was there to see us when we bolted out of the ravine and across the bare dirt of the Valley View Estates as if a bear was after us!

20 Cryptid Hunter Dudes

A bear wasn't after us. At least, it didn't follow us out of the ravine.

"It didn't really sound like a bear," Connor remembered later—in the safety of the Maguire's garage the next day.

"It didn't sound like anything from this world," said Nate, which didn't really make me feel better.

"What if it's Bigfoot?" I said, thinking of Mr. Dorminter's magazines.

"Did anybody see any footprints?" asked Ryan.

"It was too dark," said Connor.

"And we were running too fast," added Deven.

Nate read from a magazine called <u>Cryptid Facts</u>. "Sasquatch is reputed to live somewhere in the wilds of the Pacific Northwest in the dark recesses of vast tracts of land that haven't seen development."

"That doesn't sound like Sherwood Heights," I said.

"On the other hand," said Nate, "Mr. Maguire was right about the bears—I checked. They don't dance at weddings, but bears and other wild creatures *are* sometimes driven out of the wild into the suburbs."

"Maybe Bigfoot got pushed into Sherwood by those forest fires in the mountains," said Connor.

"Dudes," said Ryan, "if we've uncovered Bigfoot, we have to document our discovery."

He turned to Nate. "You said yourself there are no good pictures or videos of the legendary creature," he said. "If *we* get one, it would make *us* legendary! Plus, we still have to get our other dart."

"Lots of people have tried," I said, flipping through the clippings from Mr. Dorminter's suitcase. "But Bigfoot is always blurry or too far away from the camera."

Ryan snapped. "We need a plan to get close to him."

The rest of us looked at each other. "There's a reason why all those shots are shaky, you know," I pointed out.

"Besides, he's supposed to be stinky," added Deven, wrinkling his nose.

"You can't ask a Dude to make friends with Bigfoot just to get a selfie," said Connor.

"I don't have to," said Ryan. "Nate's got a *mechanical* Dude who can do it for us."

So, we gathered our supplies and went back to the ravine. It was hot, but the Dudes had all agreed we wanted to do this in broad daylight. This time, we had to wait until Joe's bulldozer was pointed the other way, before we crossed the construction site behind him and took the pathway through the blackberries.

We found no giant tracks or prints of bear paws. But Nate noticed a clump of short sticks jutting from the ground.

"It's as if someone cut the blackberry canes on purpose to clear a path," he said.

"Maybe Bigfoot eats blackberry canes," said Connor.

"No wonder he's so big," said Deven.

The Dudes waited at the big tree while Ryan crawled with ninja stealth further down the slope and left the robot below the big rocks.

When he returned, Nate used his Dad's old smartphone to power up the robot and direct its camera eye. We all gathered around the little screen to watch.

The robot crept forward on its tracks until it crossed the entrance to the cave.

"Hm," said Nate. "What do you notice about the floor?"

"Trash," said Deven. "Bigfoot is messy."

Ryan shrugged. "He *is* a wild animal, after all."

"No he's not," said Connor, giving his brother an elbow to the ribs, "he's a wild *person*."

Over the noise of their inevitable scuffle, Nate pointed out that the trash looked a lot like the wrappers of El Greco Granola and Mona Lisa Munchies.

"Bigfoot went to the Arts Festival?" asked Connor, disentangling himself from his brother.

"No, dufus," said Ryan. "We would have seen him."

"Not if he was disguised as Art the Owl!" suggested Deven.

Now *I* had noticed something. "The floor is pretty flat and level," I pointed out. "The robot's camera isn't even shaking as it moves."

"This is not a natural cave," Nate agreed.

Sure enough, we could see the back wall, glowing in the beam of a penlight strapped to the robot's head. There were no stalactites or stalagmites. The walls were as flat and smooth as the floor. In the corner, we could see a pile of blankets.

"Maybe that's Bigfoot's bed," said Connor.

"Dudes, does Bigfoot use tools?" asked Ryan, pointing to a set of hedge clippers leaning against the wall.

"Does Bigfoot use furniture?" I asked.

Beside the blankets was something I recognized—one of Jayden's benches, painted with Batman symbols. It was just the right size to make a bedside table for a person sleeping on the floor. And, lying on the bench, was our last Elephant dart.

"There's nobody home," declared Ryan. "Let's go get our ammo."

We all scrambled over the rocks and entered the shelter.

"Somebody's been living here all right," said Ryan. "A homeless guy, I guess."

"Bigfoot is homeless?" said Deven. "Aww! Poor thing."

"Not Bigfoot," I said. "A person."

"An artist," corrected Nate, and, as he raised a lightsaber, I could see that he was right. There were trees and leaves and animals painted all over the walls. There were pads of paper scattered around too with pretty realistic-looking nature sketches.

"Not a bad place, really," said Ryan, pocketing the dart along with the one he'd retrieved from the rocks. I guess he could appreciate someone living in what was basically a garage. At least it was cool.

"All it needs are some lawn chairs," suggested Connor.

Which is how Operation Sasquatch Selfie turned into Operation Cave Comfort. The Dudes went home and came back carrying folding chairs from Ryan and Connor's garage and the cushions from the dojo.

We had just placed a luxurious bowl of moss on the bench for decoration when Bigfoot came home.

"Oh, hi!" said Deven when he saw the man standing at the door. "We thought you were cryptic."

"He means a cryptid," Nate explained.

The stranger said nothing as he set his computer bag on the floor. He was dressed in a neat black shirt and pants and a nametag that said Sam. He stood wide-eyed as Connor leaned closer.

"You don't smell like Bigfoot," Connor confirmed. "You smell like coffee."

"Uh, thanks," said Sam. Then he squinted at Nate (who was squinting back at him through his glasses). "I know you, don't I?" he asked.

That's when I recognized him too. "That's the photographer Nate talked to at the Arts Festival," I explained.

"So Bigfoot *did* go to the arts festival!" said Deven.

"You took pictures of the old farmhouse up there before they tore it down," said Nate, pointing in the direction of the construction site.

Sam nodded. "That was my grandfather's place," he said. "I would have inherited it, but my grandfather had debts. I stayed in the farmhouse as long as I could—until the bank found a developer to buy the land."

"And Joe bulldozed it," guessed Ryan.

Sam nodded. "When they tore down the house, I had to hide out somewhere. Luckily, I knew about this old bomb shelter."

"Bomb shelter?" I asked.

And Ryan said, "I knew the mayor had a secret weapon!"

"My grandad worked up at the Hanford nuclear site during WWII," Sam explained.

"Cool!" said the Dudes together.

"Yeah, well, it left him worried about emergencies," Sam explained. "So he built this bunker—which has given me a safe place to sleep until my art career takes off."

"I have a day job at the coffee shop," he added. "That's where I charge my laptop and shaver."

Nate and I looked at each other. The electric shaver explained the strange humming noise we'd heard.

"At night I work on ideas," Sam went on, "so the city will hire me to paint a mural."

Ryan looked around the walls. "I'm not sure people are all that interested in poison ivy," he said critically.

"You should paint stuff people want to see," suggested Nate. "Explosions are good."

"How about food?" put in Connor.

"My Dad has these really artistic golf pants," Deven offered.

Sam raised his hands as if to ward us off. "Uh, thanks, guys. But I'll have to think of something on my own. At least now I can sit in a chair while I do it," he added cheerfully.

"You might want some reading material too," said Nate. He left a few copies of <u>Cryptid Facts</u> and <u>Paranormal LIFE</u> on a chair.

I guess you never know when inspiration will strike. On the last weekend of the summer, we went to the opening of the new skate park.

"They decided to call it The Wild," Nate informed us. Then he said his mom wanted him to wear a helmet just to *watch* the skateboarding.

"That might not be a bad idea," I said.

Connor had a plan to develop a new trick involving a half-cab kickflip and his dad's inner tube.

Ryan considered it a plan to break his legs.

But, when we got to the park, we found ourselves staring at an old friend. There, painted on a wall overlooking the bowl was a scene of old growth forest. And, amid the cedars and ferns, was Sasquatch, popping an ollie with fur flying. Sam's name was signed on the bottom of the cryptid's deck.

"What do you know?" said Ryan. "We got a picture of Sasquatch after all."

So summer started with a river battle and ended with Bigfoot. In between, there were a few emergencies, but I think the Dudes proved that we're prepared for anything. And that's important, because, when you're a Dude, you never know what will happen next.

THE END

Thanks for reading! If you enjoyed this book, please send the Dudes some love with a review at your favorite retailer.

Don't miss the next exciting adventure of the Dudes...

Time to multitask!

Middle school is the new high school and Dudes are low men on the totem pole. What else can they do but create a fake eighth-grader? Along the way, they:

- **Start a reality show**
- **Signal UFO's**
- **Promote devil worship**
- **And exert mind control on the student body**

But can they learn good study skills?

Don't miss the madness in:
DUDES IN THE MIDDLE

Coming soon to your favorite retailer.

Tyler Reynolds has been entrusted with the awesome duty of preserving the legend of the Dudes' epic adventures for all time. He lives with his mom and dad, two brothers, and a dog and spends his non-screen-time with his four best friends.

Check out his website at **thedudeschronicles.com**

Visit his author page on Amazon.com

Emily Kay Johnson occasionally comes out of hiding to collaborate with Tyler on the dubious project of sharing the exploits of the Dudes with the world. She lives with her husband, sons, and cats in the Pacific Northwest. She has been attacked by a bear, but she has never seen Bigfoot.

You can reach her at **EmilyKayJohnson.com**

Visit her author page on Amazon.com

Please leave a review at your favorite retailer!

Made in the USA
San Bernardino, CA
01 June 2019